A Man Named

An Exploration into the Days of Peleg

פֶּלֶג

"For in His Days
Was the Earth Divided"
—Genesis 10:25

A Man Named

An Exploration into the Days of Peleg

"For in His Days
Was the Earth Divided"
—Genesis 10:25

Clay McConkie, PhD

Portrait drawings by
John McConkie

CFI
Springville, Utah

ISBN 13: 978-1-59955-024-4

Published by CFI, an imprint of Cedar Fort, Inc., 2373 W. 700 S., Springville, UT, 84663
Distributed by Cedar Fort, Inc. www.cedarfort.com

LIBRARY OF CONGRESS CATALOGING-IN-PUBLICATION DATA

McConkie, Clay.
A man named Peleg: "for in his days was the earth divided" Genesis 10:25 / written by Clay McConkie; illustrations by John McConkie.
p. cm.
Includes bibliographical references and index.
ISBN 978-1-59955-024-4 (alk. paper)
1. Babel, Tower of. 2. Peleg (Biblical figure) 3. Bible. O.T. Genesis X-XI—Criticism, interpretation, etc. 4. Church of Jesus Christ of Latter day Saints—Doctrines. 5. Mormon Church—Doctrines. I. McConkie, John. II. Title.

BS1238.B2M42 2007
222'.1109505--dc22

2007004799

Cover design by Nicole Williams
Cover design © 2007 by Lyle Mortimer
Edited and typeset by Kimiko M. Hammari

Printed in the United States of America

10 9 8 7 6 5 4 3 2 1

Printed on acid-free paper

Note on
Repetition

It has been said that if you really want to teach something, you do it in three stages. First you tell what you are going to say, then you say it, and finally you repeat what you have just said. In other words, use plenty of repetition.

Such a saying is humorous, in a way, but it does put across an important idea. It is also reminiscent of a certain messenger who once delivered the same information to a man on three different occasions in one night and then repeated it again the next day.

In the pages that follow, considerable repetition occurs, hopefully in the correct amount and according to the right frequency. The intent is not just to present information, or put across a point or idea, but to place a strong focus upon the so-called division of the earth, an event mentioned very briefly in the Bible and one that occurred during the days of a man named Peleg.

It is also important to express the idea that when the earth was divided, there was not a geologic separation of continents creating the Eastern and Western Hemispheres, or a variety of other phenomena, but a vast deluge of water that encroached upon the earth and caused a reconfiguration of land surfaces. From the very beginning of the present discussion, this will be an important concept.

NOTE ON
Chronology

During the following account, information contained in modern scripture—namely a record known as the Doctrine and Covenants—is the primary reason for using one particular version of the Bible over any other in discussing the man named Peleg, whose birth coincided with a highly significant event in biblical history known as the division of the earth. Consequently the chronology involved is the one found in the King James Bible, and even though there are serious problems in using this particular dating system, at least for the present, the object nevertheless is to support a theory that says that things in the past happened pretty much as they are described in this version of the Bible. The intent also is to show that the earth's division, relating to the same general time period as the Tower of Babel, took place *before* the construction of the famous tower, and not *after* as commonly supposed.

An important question, however, is whether or not there was enough time between the Flood in the time of Noah and the division of the earth during the days of Peleg to develop a population large enough to build such a tower. And regardless of how events might have occurred in those days, the purpose in the following pages once more is to test the hypothesis that says that things definitely could have happened according to the conditions described in the King James chronology.

Again the main reasoning for this is that certain information in modern scripture suggests that one chronology is preferred over any other despite problems that presently exist. It is also likely that additional information will yet be discovered or revealed that will reconcile existing differences. At least the possibility of such a thing taking place is definitely there.

In addition, there is the situation pertaining to population increase during the first century following the Flood. Any demographic study on this time period is either nonexistent or difficult to obtain, and the theory and system proposed in this book, therefore, is given tenatively and very cautiously.

GENERATIONS FROM
Enoch TO *Abraham*

Enoch   Enoch was the fourth great-grandson of Adam. He and his city were taken up from the earth when he was 365 years old (Genesis 5:23-24).

Methuselah   Methuselah was the oldest man on earth and died at the age of 969, apparently during the year of the Flood (Genesis 5:27).

Lamech

Noah   The great Flood occurred in the 600th year of Noah's life (Genesis 7:6, 11).

Shem

Arphaxad

Salah

Eber   Eber was the ancestor of an important group of people (Genesis 10:21). He has been referred to as the ancestor and founder of the Hebrews.

Peleg   The earth was divided during Peleg's days. He was the third great-grandson of Noah (Genesis 10:25).

Reu

Serug

Nehor

Terah

Abraham   Abraham was the third great-grandson of Peleg (Genesis 11:26). He, in turn, was the grandfather of Jacob, who became head of the twelve tribes of Israel.

And unto Eber were born two sons: the name of one was Peleg; for in his days was the earth divided; and his brother's name was Joktan.

—Genesis 10:25

Contents

LIST OF
Illustrations

Preface

This book is a sequel to another small book I have written called *The Gathering of the Waters* in which I referred to three giant floods in history coming to an end: one on the third day of Creation, one during the time of Noah, and another yet to occur just prior to the biblical Millennium. In this second account, however, attention has mainly been given to when the floods began.

In neither book has there been any attempt to focus on floods themselves, a subject I know very little about. Instead, my main interest in the first writing was how they pertain to the lost tribes of Israel, and in the second their relationship to the division of the earth mentioned in the Bible.

From the outset, I do not claim any special status for either of these two books. But one thing I have tried to do is put forth a variety of opinions, at least some of which are hopefully closer to fact than theory. In certain things I know I could be wrong, but in others there is a good chance I am right.

An important concept in *A Man Named Peleg*, for example, is that the Tower of Babel came after the time of Peleg and the so-called division of the earth and not before, as often stated. The division, in fact, might have been the principle motive for building the tower in the first place, instead of some of the more traditional reasons. I have also emphasized the idea that the division of the earth was mainly a phenomenon pertaining to water, rather than one related to drifting continents or some other theory.

In any case, my opinions are there, and I welcome any constructive criticism. The important thing is to discover what is accurate and true. Hopefully I have made some kind of contribution, yet if I have done nothing more than stimulate additional interest in my topic, I will have accomplished a worthwhile purpose.

There is also the matter of religious faith and belief. In this second account, as well as the first, much has been said about certain events in the future, including the Second Coming of Jesus Christ, the return of the ten lost tribes of Israel, and the restoration of the earth to the way it was in the beginning before it was divided. All of these occurrences will fulfill ancient and modern prophecy and are important things to look forward to. With this in mind, I have written my two books!

Introduction

It is typical in the Bible to find isolated passages of scripture that are very brief in content yet introduce subjects of the greatest importance, conjuring up all kinds of images and ideas and raising provocative questions. "And Enoch walked with God," for example, "and he was not, for God took him".[1]

Or there is the account of Joshua giving commands to the sun and moon during a battle with the Amorites. "And the sun stood still, and the moon stayed, until the people had avenged themselves upon their enemies".[2] Obviously, it would be difficult to imagine many statements being more unusual and outstanding than these.

The same is true of a single verse in the book of Genesis. Its main purpose apparently was to document the birth of two brothers: Peleg and Joktan, the sons of Eber. This is a scripture that has often provoked only a passing thought, yet it is actually one of the most profound statements in the Bible, containing questions and implications bordering on the unbelievable!

"And unto Eber were born two sons: the name of one was Peleg; for in his days was the earth divided; and his brother's name was Joktan."[3] A companion scripture, almost identical in wording, is found in 1 Chronicles.

In very few places could there be so much meaning expressed in such a small number of words as in this last passage. The contents, very briefly stated, might seem reasonably apparent at first, yet at the same time they can very easily be misunderstood. It is as though a tremendous thought were purposely sandwiched between two relatively unimportant items of genealogy for some unknown purpose. And consequently, the passage has attracted very little attention.

It does raise some interesting questions, however, as to who Eber was, what happened to his two sons, and also what part each of them played during the historical period in which they lived (the time of the Tower of Babel and the century immediately following the great Flood).

More important is the question of what it means when it says that the earth was divided. In other words, exactly what kind of division was the ancient prophet and historian of Genesis talking about? On this last topic especially, there are many problems involved, with biblical scholars giving so many answers and solutions that any consensus of opinion at first seems unlikely.

Yet in all of the discussion and controversy, there is undoubtedly a correct answer! It is just a matter of finding it among the small amount of evidence that presently exists. And in the process of doing this, two of the people who stand out as figures of interest and importance are the two sons of Eber: Peleg and Joktan!

Figure 1

עֵבֶר

Eber

Eber had other children besides Peleg and Joktan, although they are not mentioned in the Bible. As a progenitor, however, he was singled out in scripture as an important head of family when the writer of Genesis referred to his predecessor Shem as "the father of all the children of Eber."

Possibly his most well-known designation, according to tradition, is that he was the ancestor and founder of the Hebrew people. The name Eber itself is suggestive of that claim. Especially in the book of Luke in the New Testament where he is listed as Heber, the similarity of his name to the word *Hebrew* is impressive.

Peleg AND Joktan

An interesting characteristic of these two brothers is their contrast, the different status each apparently held during his lifetime. A similar situation existed with other pairs of brothers in the Bible, such as Isaac and Ishmael, and Jacob and Esau.

It was the idea that one brother seemed to be on one path, and one on another. Each appeared to have a different calling or destiny.

As far as genealogy and the patriarchal order were concerned, for example, Peleg was the one chosen for the designated line, while Joktan was not. This might have had something to do with birthright, although as in the case of Jacob and Esau, possibly not. It is certain, however, that Peleg, along with his father, was in the long line of patriarchs that started with Adam and continued with such men as Enoch, Noah, and Abraham.

But what about Joktan? What kind of status or calling did he have, if any, and what was his destiny?

First of all, he was a man who had thirteen sons, all of whom are referred to in the Bible. Ironically, only one of Peleg's sons is mentioned, but all thirteen belonging to Joktan are listed by name.

Figure 2

יָקְטָן

Joktan

   In Joktan there is the suggestion of a younger
brother who chose a nomadic life in the desert rather
than one of farming and agriculture. As the father of
thirteen sons, he became the head of the same number
of tribes.

   Upon leaving the Mesopotamian area, he migrated
to the south where he became the originator of an
important branch of the Arabic people. The modern
tribes of southern Arabia, according to at least one
source, believe that the so-called pure Arabs are those
who descend from Joktan.

Second, the geographical area which Joktan eventually occupied appears to have been separate from that of Peleg. Each of his thirteen sons became the head of a tribe, and according to the biblical description, "their dwelling was from Mesha, as thou goest unto Sephar, a mount of the east",[4] which is generally regarded as being in the lower part of the Arabian Peninsula. It was in this locality where Joktan became the progenitor of an important branch of the Arabic people.

In contrast to this, it is probable that Peleg remained in a different area where he led a more sedentary life, possibly on irrigated land. It was also his lot, once again, to be in the chosen line, the impressive string of patriarchs which eventually led to the great prophet Abraham.

The lifestyles of the two brothers, therefore, were noticeably different, as also were the places in which they lived. In fact, their settlement in different parts of the country was just one of the phases of a large dispersion of people taking place at that time, a movement already well underway in the Middle East. This was the great scattering of nations described in the book of Genesis. Having started in the city of Babylon during the time of the Tower of Babel, it spread quickly throughout the land, and Peleg and Joktan were both part of the process!

Figure 3

פֶּלֶג

Peleg

Peleg is portrayed as someone who resided in or around ancient Mesopotamia. He probably lived at least a semi-sedentary kind of life in which he was involved in agriculture and the development of cultivation and irrigation.

In the biblical genealogies he is listed in the patriarchal line that descended from Noah and Shem. And although there is some indication in modern scripture that he was an important person, almost nothing is said about him in the pages of the Bible.

THE TOWER OF
Babel

The construction of the great tower in Babylon began sometime before or after the division of the earth that occurred during the days of Peleg. Whether it preceded or followed that event depends upon the meaning and interpretaton of the word *division*. In any case, the building is said to have had its beginning during the 23rd century BC, or several centuries earlier within the context of another chronology.

People in those days were still living in the shadow of the great Flood. Certainly they wanted nothing to do with another large deluge, and an idea uppermost in their minds was undoubtedly security. This might have been at least one of the reasons for them building such an extensive tower, with enough height at the top to "reach unto heaven."

"And they said, Go to, let us build us a city and a tower, whose top may reach unto heaven; and let us make us a name, lest we be scattered abroad upon the face of the whole earth."[5]

The Tower of Babel appears to have been the special project of Nimrod, the son of Cush and a great-grandson of the prophet Noah through his son Ham. He is the one referred to in the Bible as "a mighty hunter before the Lord",[6] and despite such a flattering description in scripture, which can be very misleading, he apparently was a very negative type of ruler, turning the people against Noah and convincing them that there might be another flood.

5

Figure 4

נִמְרֹד

Nimrod

The traditional view of Nimrod is that of a great warrior, "a mighty hunter before the Lord," according to the Bible. In actuality, however, he might have been a very despotic ruler, whose kingdom was centered in the city of Babylon.

In the biblical record there is no direct proof that Nimrod built the Tower of Babel, but tradition has it that he was definitely the one. Out of all those who lived during his time period, he is the one person who logically might have come up with such an idea.

This image of Nimrod is expressed in the writings of Josephus, the ancient Jewish historian, as well as in various other sources, including modern scripture. It portrays the character of a man who definitely was not valiant in the eyes of God, but rather one who tried to thwart God's purposes.

According to Josephus, Nimrod told his people that they were the ones responsible for their present prosperity, not God. The success and happiness they had achieved, he said, were the direct result of their own courage and industry, and it would be cowardly for them to think otherwise.

As a sign of his contempt, he threatened that if God ever thought of drowning the world again, he would respond by building a gigantic tower, the upper levels of which would be too high for floodwaters to reach. In this way, he planned not only to save himself and the people of Babylon but to gain revenge for those who had died in the great Flood as well.[7]

Also there seems to have been another reason. Construction of the tower was apparently a well-planned strategy, the design of an ambitious man who sought personal advantage and political control and would do anything to obtain them.

At least two main purposes in building the Tower of Babel, therefore, could well have been security and power. These would partially explain why the people wanted to make a name for themselves and not be scattered across the earth. Certainly it was to their advantage to be successful and politically independent. In view of this, the most important reason for the tower, as things turned out, was ostensibly that of national security, along with personal greed and power, and was Nimrod's main motive for finally going ahead with his project!

If it is true, in other words, that he told the people he would build a tower to spite God if and when a second flood seemed imminent, the thing that would logically cause him to go ahead and do such a thing would be the prospect of another flood! Any action otherwise would be just precautionary.

And theoretically that is exactly what happened! Whereas most people place the division of the earth after the Tower of Babel, associating it with the confusion of tongues and the subsequent scattering of people, or some other type of event, the more logical time would be before the tower was ever built! This suggests that the division did not pertain to any kind of population dispersion or various other possibilities, but instead to an extensive division of land caused by a huge deluge of water!

Consequently, when Nimrod heard news reports and learned that a flood of mammoth proportions was on the way, he definitely would lose no time in starting the tower. And in doing so, according to the account given by Josephus, he built it with a vengeance, "and by reason of the multitude of hands employed in it, it grew very high, sooner than anyone could expect."[8]

The decision to build the Tower of Babel, therefore, could have been prompted not so much by the memory of a previous flood, but by the apparent approach of a new one. Undoubtedly it was the subject of considerable alarm and was enough to cause immediate action!

A Variety of

Interpretations

Several meanings have been given to the statement that the earth was divided in the days of Peleg. All of these relate in one way or another to the etymology of Peleg's name, which in the Hebrew language signifies *watercourse* and *division*.

Whatever it was that happened in those days, it was an important event, enough so that Peleg was named after it. The scripture in 1 Chronicles, almost identical to the one in Genesis except for the word *because*, states very clearly the reason for such a name.

"And unto Eber were born two sons: the name of the one was Peleg because in his days the earth was divided; and his brother's name was Joktan."[9]

The important question, of course, is what is meant by the word *divided*. What happened in ancient times to prompt such an unusual term or expression? Moreover, is the event something that should be considered literally, or just figuratively or symbolically? Such a brief reference in scripture obviously creates a difficult problem, and as a consequence there are at least eleven different explanations or theories that present a possible solution.

1) The most popular theory, and the one most prevalent in the literature, is that *divided* means a division of people. This meaning is suggested early in the tenth chapter of Genesis, just

prior to the account of Peleg and Joktan's birth. Referring to Japheth, the son of Noah, the scripture reads as follows: "By these were the isles of the Gentiles divided in their lands; everyone after his tongue, after their families, in their nations."[10]

Later, only a few verses following the passage in connection with Peleg, the word *divided* is again used in the same way. "These are the families of the sons of Noah," the scripture states, "after their generations, in their nations: and by these were the nations divided in the earth after the flood."[11]

Any normal reading of Genesis in regard to these passages would likely result in one conclusion, namely that the division of the earth in the days of Peleg pertained to a division of people, both linguistically and geographically. Especially with *divided* being used three times in fairly rapid succession, the implication is that in all three instances, the same kind of event is involved, a separation and scattering of population, with the confusion of tongues at the Tower of Babel being a principle factor.

2) Another interpretation of the word in question is that it refers to the time when Peleg and Joktan separated and went their different ways. When the latter left his homeland to migrate southward into the Arabian Peninsula, for example, he took his thirteen sons with him, and there they became the leaders of thirteen different tribes. Peleg, in the meantime, apparently remained in the Mesopotamian area, with the result being that a significant division occurred among the people, more specifically within the family of Eber.

Since Eber is traditionally considered to be the progenitor of the Hebrews, the separation of his two sons who are mentioned by name in the Bible certainly could be interpreted as a dividing point, Peleg continuing on in the patriarchal line, and Joktan establishing a well-known ethnic group called the Joktanide Arabs. Like Isaac and Ishmael later on, and also Jacob and Esau, these two brothers represented important milestones in history, each playing a vital part in the development of nations in the Middle East.

3) A third explanation of the word *divided* pertains to a political and geographical division of territory. It might have involved the establishment of certain types of territorial limits or municipal boundaries, but whatever it was, if it actually happened during Peleg's time, it evidently had an important impact on a large population of people.

4) In contrast to these theories, there is also the idea that the division of the earth referred more accurately to irrigation and agriculture. The etymology of Peleg's name, in fact, has to do with water as well as division. Associated with the origin of the word are such meanings as watercourse, canal, and channel, and the earth in those early days might have been thought of as being divided when people in Mesopotamia began building extensive irrigation canals.

Peleg's birth possibly coincided with agricultural innovations that were significant enough to warrant his family giving him a special name. Certainly few things were more important than water at that time, and when irrigation canals began crisscrossing the countryside, where earlier there had been only unproductive land, it could naturally have been regarded as a unique event, enough so that more persons than one might have been given the name of Peleg.

5) Another meaning of the word *divided* is that it was the conclusion of the great Flood during the time of Noah. Instead of water rapidly draining off from the earth, as recorded in the Bible, it is suggested that it subsided more slowly, continuing until the days of Peleg at which time the division of land into islands and continents finally became complete.

6) Along with these explanations, some minor ones also exist, including (a) a mystical interpretation pertaining to the separation of the sexes, (b) the point in the development of man when he realized that his material or physical nature was separate from his inner spiritual self, (c) a separation of mankind into different groups because of quarrels and dissensions, even before the Tower of Babel, and (d) a dividing point in history

when people's life spans became significantly shortened.

7) Finally, and in addition to all of these, there are still two other theories that pertain to a division of the earth, both relatively minor as far as their prevalence in the literature is concerned, yet one of them possibly being the explanation that comes closest to the truth. The first refers to a breakup in the earth's original landmass as described in the theory of continental drift, while the other involves a gigantic deluge of water, a second flood in close succession to the one before it, which inundated large sections of land and created present-day islands and continents.

Both of these views, characterized by highly physical phenomena, differ markedly with most of the other explanations, as well as with one another. Each presents a very different idea as to what happened when the earth's land surface was divided in the days of Peleg. Yet when everything is considered, one view shows a definite advantage over the other, especially in regard to chronology and certain principles of modern-day science!

Two Important
Theories

The continental drift theory states that the lower half of Africa's western coast at one time adjoined the eastern coast of South America, and also that the rest of Africa connected mainly with the eastern part of North America. Other sections of the earth were joined together in a similar way, all forming one landmass. Then came a time when the land started drifting apart to form continents, continuing to do so until it arrived at the condition in which it appears today. This theory at present is generally a well-accepted concept and is referred to in the scientific community as plate tectonics.

There is a time problem, however, in associating the drifting continents with what took place during the days of Peleg. Scientists estimate that landforms started moving sometime between 200 and 300 million years ago, whereas Bible chronologists place Peleg's time at about 2250 BC, or possibly a few centuries earlier according to a different chronology.

Of course, it could be said that in this instance, due to divine intervention, things happened much more quickly. There are those places in scripture, for example, that suggest that rapid changes in geology sometimes occur but are later attributed to long passages of time.

Also one might say that science has been wrong before, and in this case it could be wrong again. And yet in regard to this particular situation, it probably would be well to avoid

Figure 5

Drifting Continents

Piecing together the parts of a world map might give a general idea of what the earth looked like more than 200 million years ago after the continents started drifting apart.

Alfred Wegener, the man who brought the continental drift theory into prominence, gave his concept of the original landmass the name of Pangaea.

conflict between an important biblical event and a popular scientific idea. Besides, another explanation and one that is much more applicable to the time of Peleg definitely exists.

This last theory is one that is supported by both ancient and modern scripture and at the same time is more acceptable in terms of science. It is the idea of water coming in upon the earth via rainfall and underground sources, at least one of these and maybe both, inundating large areas of land and causing a mammoth division of territory. It was very similar to what happened earlier during the great Flood, except now the incoming water was far less extensive. Whereas complete inundation might have occurred in the first instance, only a partial one took place in the second.

It was also a deluge that was separate and distinct from the one just before it. And although the idea of two major floods occurring so close to one another might at first seem improbable, there are good reasons for believing that such a thing definitely did happen.

In comparison with continental drift, therefore, this kind of explanation is much more likely to avoid an unnecessary confrontation between scientific theory and the Bible, as well as present a logical view of what actually took place. It is also an idea which is more tenable as far as the etymology of Peleg's name is concerned. And the one main clue in reaching these conclusions is found in a very unexpected place, hidden in a remote and secluded location in the literature! Very brief in content, it occurs suddenly and unexpectedly, much like its companion material in the Bible.

There are only two verses in biblical scripture, for example, one in Genesis and the other in 1 Chronicles, that mention the division of the earth during the days of Peleg. Extremely brief and ambiguous, they have long been a puzzle to biblical scholars and have often created a very difficult problem. Ironically, there is the same number of verses in a book of modern-day scripture, just as brief in wording and content, that refer to this same event. And it is this last piece of information, found in a record called the Doctrine and Covenants endorsed by The Church of Jesus Christ of Latter-day Saints, that finally unravels the mystery of what the account in the Bible pertaining to a division actually means.

Besides explaining the word *divided*, relating it specifically to a large deluge of water, these two verses of scripture not only establish the cause of the deluge but also reveal its geographical source as well!

Referring to the latter days and the Second Coming of Jesus Christ, the verses read as follows: "He shall command the great deep, and it shall be driven back into the north countries, and the islands shall become one land. And the land of Jerusalem and the land of Zion shall be turned back into their own place, and the earth shall be like as it was in the days before it was divided."[12]

This one scripture, providing valuable information and insight, answers several puzzling questions. First, the division of the earth during Peleg's time was the result of incoming water, an extreme flooding of land that created the configuration of hundreds of islands and seven continents.

Second, the statement that water was "driven back into the north countries" is a strong implication that this is where the water came from in the first place, originating somewhere in the northern part of the globe, apparently in places of outlet permitting the effluence of huge amounts of subterranean water. It came down from the north, and it will someday go back into the north. Within the context of this scripture, water "gathered together unto one place," as described in the biblical account of Creation, takes on a different kind of significance, or at least a double meaning and second interpretation.

Third, it is especially important, after the many opinions that have been given, to learn more about the word *divided* as it is used in the books of Genesis and 1 Chronicles. To some it might be a small thing, but for others, it stands as a unique and outstanding discovery. There appears to be considerable evidence now that the word in question refers to a significant deluge during the days of Peleg, reminiscent of the time of Creation and the great Flood in the days of Noah. And confirmation of this is once again found in the remarkable scripture recorded in the book known as the Doctrine and Covenants!

GATHERING OF THE
Waters

The idea of a separate flood during Peleg's time is related to a concept that might be referred to as the gathering of the waters, something that has occurred twice so far in the world's recorded history and is yet to occur a third time in the last days. It is an extraordinary and supernatural phenomenon and is documented in both ancient and modern scripture.

The concept is first mentioned during the account of Creation in the opening chapter of Genesis. And although the phraseology is familiar to anyone acquainted with the Bible, the impact of the words when read carefully can be overwhelming and almost unbelievable.

"And the earth was without form, and void; and darkness was upon the face of the deep. And the Spirit of God moved upon the face of the waters.

"And God said, Let the waters under the heaven be gathered together unto one place, and let the dry land appear: and it was so. And God called the dry land Earth; and the gathering together of the waters called he Seas: and God saw that it was good."[13]

In connection with these events, the implication is that the earth at one time was completely covered by a vast ocean, the result of a giant flood. At some point during the creation process, enough water came from somewhere to cover the entire globe, the suggestion being that it originated in areas beneath the earth's surface.

Or maybe it was more simplified than that. In other words, when the earth was set into place, and was without form, and void, the water was already there.

Whatever it was that happened, the planet eventually ended up with a liquid surface. Then came the command on the third day of Creation for reducing or displacing a huge amount of water in order to create dry land. In the terminology of the Bible, "the waters were gathered together." This was a tremendous undertaking, one that lasted several months if compared with the great Flood in Noah's time, or an untold number of centuries according to a broader view, and it brings up an inevitable question. And that is, what happened to the large volume of ocean that disappeared or that was possibly relocated?

A supernatural event in which water simply vanished could be the answer. When Jesus fed the five thousand, for example, there was a miraculous increase or multiplication of food, and according to some kind of reverse principle, either food or water might be quickly and miraculously reduced.

Another possibility is that widespread sinking of terrain occurred, allowing water to rush into low places and at the same time causing surrounding landforms to appear. This type of occurrence, however, would only result in water displacement rather than any kind of reduction, unless much of the water flushed down into underground areas of the earth.

Finally, at least one other possible answer exists. It is suggested in the Genesis account where water is described as gathering unto one place. Of course, one place could mean that all the water ended up in one area and the land in another, yet there might also be a second interpretation, or at least a double meaning. A strong implication is given that a tremendous mass of ocean was actually drawn to a specific geographical location somewhere in the north, after which a uniform sea level by some kind of natural phenomenon was established and maintained.

This last idea, which at first might seem unlikely and impractical, even supernatural, could conceivably be closer to the truth than any other theory. Certainly it is the idea in modern scripture that refers to the return of floodwaters that allegedly originated in Peleg's time. Also it could be the same type of phenomenon that occurred following the catastrophic deluge in the days of Noah.

In the great Flood especially, there is the example of how a huge body of water can appear very suddenly, covering the earth in a relatively short time and then quickly go back again, apparently returning to an original source. Such a massive appearance and disappearance of ocean would be more than impressive. But an important idea is that the water action might have been according to a pre-established pattern in which floodwaters came down from the north and then returned to their former place.

The implication of such a thing happening is definitely there. In any case, whatever it was that took place during Noah's time, at least, turned out to be an extremely significant event, as well as a tragic one, and it initiated a brand new era in the world's history. It also acquainted mankind with the circumstances of a giant deluge and proved to everyone what it was like to have a devastating flood!

THE GREAT
Flood

T he deluge that covered the earth in the time of Noah and caused such widespread destruction apparently came from two main sources: rainfall and subterranean water. It seems logical that most of it came from below rather than above, considering how much water there was, but the important thing is that while it rained for 150 days, water was also coming in from underground areas.

"In the six hundredth year of Noah's life, in the second month, the seventeenth day of the month, the same day were all the fountains of the great deep broken up, and the windows of heaven were opened. . . . And the waters prevailed upon the earth an hundred and fifty days."[14] At this point both the rain and the underground flooding came to an end!

Whether or not the earth was completely submerged has been debated, but the biblical record does state that all the high hills and mountains were covered and that all living things upon the earth were killed. Although other reasons are given in support of complete inundation, these two are the traditional ones.

No mention is made of any natural phenomena that contributed to the Flood except rainfall and the flooding from underground sources. If there were any, at least they are not mentioned specifically in the Bible.[15] It was mainly the release of a huge volume of water that possibly came and went in much the same way.

One thing is certain. The giant deluge in the days of Noah was one of the most dramatic events in human history, and the subsequent withdrawal of water during a period of about five or five and a half months was in some ways no less spectacular.

An important question, however, is whether or not the subterranean water actually went back the same way it came. And although there is no definite answer, logic once again would say yes.

It is a type of water action that consists of two parts. Part one during the great Flood was water coming by way of rainfall and underground sources. Part two was the water returning to those sources, or in other words, gathering the waters together and causing the dry land to appear.

The underground sources, of course, were the mysterious phenomena in the Bible referred to briefly as the fountains of the great deep!

FOUNTAINS OF THE

I n very few places in the biblical record is there a reference to fountains of the deep or fountains of the great deep. Yet these small scriptures, almost lost in a maze of verses, imply something very remarkable: somewhere beneath the earth's surface, huge reservoirs or underground caverns exist that have a capacity for holding an almost unfathomable amount of water!

It is this phenomenon of the fountains, surrounded by mystery down through the ages, that theoretically holds the key to mammoth floods and the gathering of waters. Very possibly it is the giant water supply for the mysterious place in the north where large deluges emerge and then go back again after spreading out across the earth's surface.

Although there are only a few places in the Bible where the fountains are specifically mentioned, the location and function of such an unusual area make it extremely important. First, it was evidently the main source of water during the Flood, rather than rainfall. The world record for rain in one day is 73.6 inches, and if that figure is multiplied by 150 days of rain, it amounts to 920 feet. Using this total as an approximation of the rainwater involved, it appears obvious that the remaining quantity of water necessary to cover even a few of the hills and mountains of the earth would be much greater. A tremendous amount would have had to come from subterranean sources.

Figure 6

Records for Rainfall

World

One Day	73.62 inches
	March 15 and 16, 1952
	Cilaos, La Reunion, Indian Ocean
One Month	366 inches
	July, 1861
	Cherrapunji, Meghalaya, India
One Year	1,041.8 inches
	August 1, 1860 to July 31, 1861
	Cherrapunji, Meghalaya, India

United States

One Day	19 inches
	July 25 and 26, 1979
	Alvin, Texas
One Year	739 inches
	December, 1981 to December, 1982
	Kukui, Maui, Hawaii
One Year	184.56 inches
	Continental United States
	1931
	Wynoochee Oxbow, Washington

*Peter Matthews, ed., *The Guinness Book of Records, 1994* (New York: Guinness Publishing Company, 1993), 23.

Second, the fountain outlets might have been at any number of places on the ocean floor or even on land surfaces, but more particularly, depending on scriptural interpretation, at one specific geographic location. This has been designated in modern scripture as a region in the northern part of the globe.[16] It could be the same general area as the north country or the land of the north spoken of by the prophet Jeremiah, and the place also where the lost tribes of Israel disappeared many centuries ago.

Third, in the same place in modern scripture, as well as in the Bible, the fountains seem to be given an equal status with three other great creations: the heavens, the earth, and the sea. "And the servants of God shall go forth, saying with a loud voice: Fear God and give glory to him, for the hour of his judgment is come; and worship him that made heaven, and earth, and the sea, and the fountains of waters."[17]

The term "fountains of waters" might be interpreted as a variety of water features on the earth's surface, including rivers, lakes, and streams. And yet the fact that it is listed with three other creations of the greatest importance suggests that it is much more than this. A more logical conclusion would be that this object of nature constitutes a major entity, along with the heavens, the earth, and the sea, and is synonymous with the fountains of the great deep in the Bible.

The important thing, of course, is the idea of subterranean water and the implication in scripture that somewhere beneath the earth's surface it does exist. If the account of the Flood in the book of Genesis is to be taken at its word, such water exists in mammoth proportions.

When the fountains of the deep were broken up during the time of Noah, it was as though all nature had broken loose, and as a result of the earth being flooded with water, an era of world history came to an end as an entire race of people was almost totally destroyed!

THREE GIANT

Deluges

It is not so much a question of whether or not the fountains exist, therefore, but rather where they are located. Also in what area of the globe, or in what different geographic places, would the emergence of subterranean water most likely occur?

Obviously, people could speculate indefinitely on this kind of topic without ever coming to any agreement of opinion. References to fountains of the deep are another good example of scripture that might create a problem and at the same time give little or no clues for a solution.

The best possibility for an answer, however, and one that suggests a general location for the influx of a huge amount of subterranean water, not only during the great Flood but also at the time of Creation and the division of the earth, might well be the two small verses of modern scripture tucked away in a very remote place in the literature: "He shall command the great deep, and it shall be driven back into the north countries, and the islands shall become one land; and the land of Jerusalem and the land of Zion shall be turned back into their own place, and the earth shall be like as it was in the days before it was divided."[18]

If it can be established from this single scripture that the deluge that allegedly took place during the days of Peleg came out of the north countries and will someday return to the same geographic area, it can then be hypothesized that a similar situation occurred at the time of Creation and also the Flood. One concept of flooding, that is, would be more logical than three different ones. This means that all of these phenomena comprise a two-part process where water comes from some vast subterranean region related to the north country and then eventually goes back again to its original source.

Because such a theory rests almost entirely on two verses of scripture, it might be argued that its validity is suspect and questionable. Yet the new information which it reveals is still plausible enough to give the theory considerable credibility. Along with the supporting evidence from the book of Genesis, it now provides important insight into previously unanswered questions and generates some very interesting implications.

1) At one point during the beginning of Creation, a gigantic flood covered the globe, emerging from a subterranean outlet in the north. Three days later, in terms of biblical time, part of the floodwater was gathered together again unto the same place where it was absorbed back into underground areas.

2) The fountains of the deep that were broken up during the great Flood in the days of Noah also had their main outlet somewhere in the north countries. The tremendous volume of water that they produced inundated the earth and once more eventually returned to the place where it had originated.

3) In the time of Peleg, water again came down from the north, encroaching more slowly upon the land this time, and yet fast enough to cause Nimrod to build the Tower of Babel.

4) Finally, during the latter days, when an important phase of world history draws to a close, floodwaters for a third time will return to their original source, and the earth's surface will become like it was before it was divided. At that time a huge landmass will run continuously for thousands of miles in every direction. It will be surrounded by a much lesser amount of water, and instead of there being continents and smaller areas of territory like today, the land surface of the globe will be comparable to one gigantic island.

This last gathering of the waters, the reverse action of the influx which occurred in Peleg's time, is particularly important, not only because it helps solve the division of the earth problem, but it is also a strong indication of what happened at the time of Creation and during the great Flood. In addition, it adds credibility to the idea that the earth's giant deluges are all interrelated, each one occurring according to the same general pattern and coming out of the same geographic area!

A Subterranean
Theory

One of the difficulties in developing a view or concept in relation to mammoth floods is justifying the possibility of huge amounts of subterranean water. Whether or not geologists and earth scientists would ever agree with this type of thing is questionable, at least in regard to the large quantities that are suggested.

If the earth during the Creation was completely inundated, for example, and then enough water was drawn off to create land surfaces, the amount of receding water must have been comparable to an underground sea or ocean. This suggests that in the very beginning, before the earth ever had a liquid surface, a gigantic volume of water existed in subterranean reservoirs.

In connection with such an idea, it is interesting to note a commentary by Robert Davidson, at one time an instructor in Old Testament Language and Literature at the University of Glasgow. While discussing the third day of Creation, he quotes Psalm 24:2 as it is translated in the New English Bible: "For it was he who founded it upon the seas and planted it firm upon the waters beneath."

The King James Version of the Bible gives a similar description of the same verse: "For he hath founded it upon the seas, and established it upon the floods."

The commentary by Professor Davidson then follows. "From other Old Testament passages," he says, "it is clear that the earth is regarded as a solid disk founded upon the subterranean waters which surface in the seas."[19]

This kind of interpretation, representative of how people in antiquity sometimes viewed the makeup of the earth, is different from any modern view, of course, yet ironically it is suggests how things might actually be, at least to a certain degree. It could be one of those times when ancient culture, even mythology, again sheds important light upon the truth.

If the waters during Creation were gathered unto one place, for example, and then engineered into some other area of the earth where they had been located earlier, it implies once more that the planet's surface was originally undermined by huge seas and oceans.[20] And when the time came for mammoth deluges to occur, not only the one in the beginning but the two that took place during the days of Noah and Peleg, those underground areas in some way released an incredible amount of water, which eventually was destined to return to its source once the floods were over.

A subterranean theory, therefore, specifically as it relates to the fountains of the deep, stands as a very logical view as to how floods originate. Certainly there are other possibilities,[21] but this is the explanation that comes very close to meeting the different criteria mentioned in modern scripture and the Bible. Possibly more than any other theory, it gives a reasonable view of what happened during each of the three deluges, and of two of them in particular: the giant deluge that almost destroyed the world in the time of Noah and the one which allegedly occurred in the days of Peleg!

IMPORTANT
Clues

Very few events in history can compare with that of the great Flood. When it comes to natural disasters, it has no equal, especially if the account in the Bible is taken seriously. It was also one of the important divisions of all time as far as the biblical patriarchs were concerned, separating Adam and Enoch on one side from Abraham and Moses on the other, with the prophet Noah in between.

Surely there is not enough that can be said about this outstanding event. Its tremendous magnitude and the terrible impact it had on the people of the ancient world are well documented in history. Along with the biblical account, there are many other versions of what happened, legends and stories coming down from the past, and although very different in some ways, they all point to a time when a great deluge did occur.

And out of all of these accounts, there is none more poignant and vivid than one originating in Babylonia in which Utnapishtim, the counterpart of Noah, describes briefly what he saw.

"It was terrible," he said. "All light was turned to darkness. The rains poured down. The storm raged, like a battle charge on mankind. The boat trembled. The gods wept. I looked out upon the sea. All mankind was turned to clay, like logs floating about."[22]

Because the Flood is remembered as such a great destruction and calamity, it continues to be a reminder that someday similar upheavals could happen again. In the account recorded in the Bible, a cautionary tone is expressed on every page. Yet along with all of this, there is also another aspect of the text, one that goes beyond the Flood itself and gives important information on what might cause deluges in the first place.

It suggests that from the very beginning, the earth was created in such a way as to accommodate large movements of water without necessarily requiring extensive land changes. There was a built-in capacity for floods, as it were. Only twice, and maybe three times, in recorded history have giant deluges taken place, but when they have, the machinery for them has been ready. And in the Flood account found in the book of Genesis, it gives a good idea of how things might have happened.

The existence of incoming water for 150 days, for example, was a significant factor and also a strong support for the theory of subterranean reservoirs. If theories such as tidal waves and rising and sinking terrain are used to explain what happened, not nearly as many days would be required to do what was necessary. Any of these kinds of phenomena might have accomplished things in a much shorter time. But to bring up the amount of underground water needed to cover the entire earth, or at least a large portion of it, is another matter. A full 150 days certainly would not be out of the question. The length of the incoming flood, therefore, might well indicate the type of water action that was involved.

A second factor suggesting subterranean water is the amount of time it took for the Flood to subside. Five months were required for the waters to move in upon the earth and five or five and a half more for them to move out. This would imply a slow and more natural function of nature, rather than the reversal of some kind of physical alteration on land surfaces or on ocean floors, although some of this might also have taken place.

Finally, and in connection with these two factors, it is a certain phrasing of language in the Bible that provides another important clue. This is the statement that all the fountains of the great deep were "broken up." Theoretically, such wording could refer to any number of things, including the occurrence of massive earthquakes and tidal waves, but a strong indication is that there was some kind of fracturing in the earth permitting subterranean water to surface. Extensive flooding came from below, in other words, at the same time that rain was falling from above.

Each of these factors points to one main conclusion: Instead of sinking land surfaces, rising ocean floors, tidal waves, or other such phenomena, all of which might have occurred to some degree, it was mainly a huge upsurge of water from underground areas that inundated the earth during the great Flood. Other factors could have played a part, but they are not mentioned in the Bible. Allegedly the deluge came and went in the same way, going through the same basic process as during the time of Creation and according to one that was to happen again in the future, starting with the time of Peleg.

Along with this information, however, there is still a problem regarding subterranean water and the fountains of the deep. It pertains to the phrase "all the fountains," and especially the word *all*, which implies that large ruptures occurred not just in one location but at various places around the globe. These openings, similar to breaks in a water main, could have precipitated a flood in many different areas simultaneously. And certainly that is a picture that comes to mind.

Yet there is a strong argument against this concept, and one which opens up an entirely new theory and possibility. It is the idea suggested in modern scripture that all three of the earth's deluges, at least the one in Peleg's time, came from somewhere in the north. Floodwaters emerged from a source that is presently unknown, but the path that the water followed as it spread out across the earth definitely came from a northern location!

Somewhere in a northern place, in some far corner of the earth, subterranean water came to the surface and caused vast flooding across the land. No mention is made of anything coming from the south or any other direction, only from a place in the northern part of the globe.

If it were not for this single source of information in modern scripture, important questions relating to the great Flood and also the division of the earth would still be matters of speculation. Instead of there being just one interpretation, which has a considerable amount of credibility, there would continue to be several, each one presenting a logical solution yet at the same time very possibly bypassing the truth. But as it is now, there is a completely different viewpoint, a new matrix or framework, within which to view information pertaining to the deluges, and particularly the one in the days of Peleg that appears to have emerged from an undetermined location situated somewhere in the north countries!

The North

Countries

The so-called land of the north, or the north countries, has long been one of the places of mystery in the Bible. Mentioned especially by the prophets Jeremiah and Ezekiel, its boundaries were undetermined. The north countries could have referred not just to one place but to any number of different geographical areas.

Sometimes it clearly indicates places of captivity in Assyria and Babylonia, whereas other times it suggests a region far beyond. Gog, for example, the one who will lead a host of armies against Israel in the future Battle of Armageddon, is supposed to come out of the land of Magog in the "north parts." This is an area that the historian Josephus associated with ancient Scythia, located near the upper parts of the Black and Caspian Seas.

A place even more remote than this, however, is one referred to in connection with the lost tribes of Israel who disappeared in the north countries many centuries ago. In fact, when the time comes for these tribes to return someday, it is said that their reentry into modern society will be accompanied by miraculous circumstances, including an unusual fracturing of rock and an avalanche of ice which will "flow down at their presence."[23] Such statements, of course, hint at a place much further to the north.

Figure 7

The Land of the North
or the North Countries

A specific geographic location is not always clear when the scriptures refer to the north countries or the land of the north. Depending on the situation, there might be several different possibilities, three of which are indicated above.

The north countries, therefore, might pertain to several different locations, ranging anywhere from ancient Mesopotamia to the vicinity of northern Asia. But in their connection with floods, and a possible gathering place of the waters, a remote region is definitely implied. Modern scripture in particular suggests an area far to the north, even close to the Arctic Circle or the polar regions beyond.

Wherever this place might be, it is clearly a place of mystery. Not only is it associated with the lost tribes of Israel and the mysterious land of Magog and Armageddon, but it is also the alleged point of exit for a massive amount of subterranean water. Somewhere in the north, a strategic water system apparently exists, a huge hydraulic network that permits gigantic floods to emerge from beneath the earth's surface and then, when a deluge comes to an end, return again to the same place where it is engineered back into underground areas.

Such a theory would pertain not just to one flood but three, establishing a similar pattern for all. It would explain each of the great deluges mainly by way of subterranean water, rather than any spectacular upheaval of nature or extensive land changes.

Again this is not to say that upheavals do not occur at the time of a deluge. In the future, in fact, when the final floodwaters recede, a time is scheduled when "every mountain and hill will be made low" and rough places will become plain. Other such phenomena are also predicted. But when the scriptures speak of such things as the earth being divided in the days of Peleg or of islands fleeing and being "moved out of their places" in the last days, a deluge rather than geological change is implied, water coming in upon the land in one instance and then receding again in the other.

In view of this, therefore, the theory that floods originate at a subterranean level and then surface in the north countries represents a significant idea and concept, one that has the potential to answer a large number of questions. And as precarious as it might sound sometimes, it could very well be the truth, or at least very close to it. If this kind of phenomenon is true, it should be no harder to accept than certain other miraculous events, many of which have long been recorded in the Bible.

The reality is that no one knows the absolute truth about certain things, and that is why they continue to be theories. But when enough evidence accumulates in favor of a particular idea, it is common sense to look into it!

A New

Concept

After all that has been said about the division of the earth, the problem of its interpretation and meaning, it is possible there will never be a satisfactory solution without the help of additional information, including new scripture. Unless this type of material is used, speculation will likely continue with little or no signs of agreement.

As a result of modern scripture, however, it can now be stated that the division probably refers to a large deluge of water that encroached upon the earth during the third millennium BC, or according to a different chronology, a short time earlier. This deluge divided the land into a network of continents and islands. Prior to that time, land surfaces were allegedly a single mass of territory running thousands of miles in every direction and fronting upon a much smaller amount of sea and ocean.

This new concept of the division of the earth not only describes the flood in Peleg's time but implies important data concerning the other two deluges as well. They, in turn, add their own information, with the result being a different kind of view that has not previously existed.

To begin with, the concept of the division of the earth consists of four main ideas: (1) Floodwaters came from one location somewhere in the north countries and will someday return, being "driven back" to the same area. (2) It was mainly

41

subterranean water that was involved, surging up in certain regions of the north and then flowing southward onto land surfaces. On its return in the future it will be absorbed back into underground areas where it originated. (3) The flood was a two-part process in which water will return to its source in basically the same way that it came. (4) A divine command is to be given at the time the deluge ends, which suggests that one was also given in the days of Peleg when it began.

As it turns out, two of these ideas also pertain to the deluge that took place at the time of Creation. During that earlier period, for example, when "darkness was upon the face of the deep," a divine commandment was given for the waters to be gathered together, and the gathering area was referred to as being at one place, possibly in the north. In addition, subterranean water and a two-part process are suggested, although not stated directly.

In regard to the great Flood, there are again two similarities. A two-part process occurred in which floodwaters apparently came and went in the same way, and subterranean water definitely appears to have been the main factor, although geologic factors might also have existed. No reference is made to any divine command, but a seven-day warning was given before the deluge started, and a wind passed over the earth when it was time for the flood to end.

Finally, there is one more idea that characterizes the division of the earth, and also possibly sets it apart from the other two floods that preceded it. It is related to the question of how long it took for the deluge during Noah's time to recede.

The standard established in the great Flood was five months for water to come from subterranean levels and five or five and a half more for it to return. Geologic changes are not mentioned in the Bible and may have been unnecessary, at least as far as water movement was concerned, everything happening according to a natural process similar to putting water into a tub and then draining it. In connection with the Creation, water action might have been much the same way.

Figure 8

Characteristics of the Three Deluges

Creation

1. Divine Command
2. Water Gathered to One Place
   (Subterranean water and a two-part process are implied.)

The Great Flood

1. Two-Part Process
2. Subterranean Water
   (A divine command is implied.)

Days of Peleg

1. Divine Command
2. Water Gathered to One Place
3. Subterranean Water
4. Two-part Process

Yet in relation to the division of the earth, the situation in the future could turn out very differently. In the last days, at a time when many concluding events are scheduled to occur, things might happen during a much shorter time period. The return of the flood that originated in the days of Peleg, whose influx was possibly several months or longer, could very well take place in the future much more quickly and unexpectedly.

The occasion will be in the vicinity of the Second Coming of Jesus Christ, the time when he appears and personally ushers in the Millennium. It will be in the days of the Battle of Armageddon and also when the ten lost tribes of Israel return. Moreover, this will be at a time when all of the world's regular history is consummated and brought to an end, after which the earth finally will be renewed and restored to the way it was in the beginning.

It is this last time period that is dramatically described in a book of modern scripture. And in addition to the two verses that specifically refer to a division of the earth and a final gathering of waters, there are those that give additional information and paint a very vivid picture of the Lord's Second Coming!

"For behold, he shall stand upon the mount of Olivet, and upon the mighty ocean," the scripture says, "even the great deep, and upon the islands of the sea, and upon the land of Zion. And he shall utter his voice out of Zion, and he shall speak from Jerusalem, and his voice shall be heard among all people; and it shall be a voice as the voice of many waters, and as the voice of a great thunder, which shall break down the mountains, and the valleys shall not be found.

"He shall command the great deep, and it shall be driven back into the north countries, and the islands shall become one land; and the land of Jerusalem and the land of Zion shall be turned back into their own place, and the earth shall be like as it was in the days before it was divided. And the Lord, even the Savior, shall stand in the midst of his people, and shall reign over all flesh.

"And they who are in the north countries shall come in remembrance before the Lord; and their prophets shall hear his voice, and shall no longer stay themselves; and they shall smite the rocks, and the ice shall flow down at their presence."[24]

Such occurrences as these, similar to God gathering the waters together and Joshua commanding the sun and moon to stand still, might easily be regarded as incomprehensible and unbelievable. They are events so far removed from everyday experience that when people first hear about them, their reaction is often very skeptical.

For some, a first inclination might be to accept them merely because they are scriptural, while others reject them outright, either because they believe the scripture not to be canonical or not scripture at all. In any case, a person might be unsure, and the truth of something hangs in the balance for a time.

Someone is being honest, however, when he admits he has doubts, when he says there are certain things that are too difficult to accept. Undoubtedly, for many people some of the miracles in the Bible are of this type. A young child might accept them as truth, but as a person gets older, he sometimes develops what he regards as a more practical or realistic point of view.

The difficulty is trying to avoid gullibility on the one hand and accepting truth, despite its questionable appearance, on the other. Certain ideas pertaining to the division of the earth and the gathering of waters are definitely good examples, and there is no surprise when such ideas are not readily accepted.

But truth is truth and will not go away. Often it is elusive and hidden, but it is always there. It is just a matter of consistently searching for it and finding it!

If there is such a thing as subterranean water coming out of the north countries, for example, and then returning again, that knowledge will someday be revealed. If the division of the earth was caused by a giant flood instead of some other type of event, that too will become known. In the meantime, it is a matter of giving thought and consideration, of doing research and investigation, testing different ideas to see if they are valid and consistent and then making at least a tentative decision on what is real, and eventually what is true.

And as far as the man named Peleg is concerned, whose name and origin are always in the background in regard to these occurrences, he also will be revealed someday. After more than four thousand years, his true character and identity will finally be made known. As it is now, he continues only as a puzzle and a mystery.

Who he was and what kind of role he played are still very much in question. Modern scripture does refer to him as "a great man," but there is no further information about him beyond what little is found in the Bible.

Yet one thing is clearly stated. And that is that Peleg was someone who definitely did exist, the son of Eber and the brother of Joktan, and also a direct descendant of the prophet Noah. He was a man who lived in or around Mesopotamia and was part of the patriarchal line. In addition, he was also the one who happened to be born at a very unexpected crossroad in time and consequently ended up as the namesake of a unique and mysterious event in world history!

Peleg
AND *Noah*

An investigation of the theory relating to Peleg and the division of the earth goes back almost to the beginning of the Bible, to the tenth chapter of Genesis where it speaks of Eber's two sons. "The name of one was Peleg," the text says, "for in his days was the earth divided; and his brother's name was Joktan."[25]

Nothing is said about Peleg after that, except that he lived 239 years according to one chronology and 339 according to another, and begat sons and daughters, including a son named Reu. The names of his father and ancestors and some of his descendants are given, but that is it. And so the question might well be asked again: Who was the one that the scriptures mention so briefly and whose name is associated with such an important biblical event? Exactly who was the man named Peleg?

Obviously, he was someone who so far has received a great deal of attention, considering what little is known about him. His only claim to fame, so to speak, beyond his genealogical status and his position in the patriarchal line, is that his birth or early lifetime coincided with the time that the earth was divided.

That is the sum of it, and the full extent of his identity. And yet at the same time, and in some ways, it is enough.

Although he is a figure almost lost in obscurity, for example, he is nevertheless an important factor in solving the mystery surrounding the so-called division of the earth. Along with his name being used for reference and terminology, he is a main focal point around which many issues can be analyzed and discussed.

Yet still he might be even more than that. And maybe the best way of gaining additional clues and insight concerning him is through what might have been his most famous contemporary, the prophet Noah.

It is Noah who is the oldest man recorded in the Bible except for Jared and Methuselah. Although he was 600 years old at the time of the Flood, he continued to live three and a half centuries after that. That was long enough to have descendants who were five generations beyond him, one of whom was Peleg, a third great-grandson. In fact, it could conceivably have been Noah himself who gave Peleg his famous name at the time of the earth's division, considering the unusual importance of the occasion.

All of this depends, of course, on the conditions of chronology and also upon where the two men were living at the time. According to one dating system, such as that found in the King James Version of the Bible, a total of 101 years elapsed between the great Flood and the birth of Peleg. In another system, however, that of the Septuagint or Greek version of the Old Testament, the same span of time comprises 531 years, including an added generation. Since Noah lived 350 years beyond the Flood, according to both chronologies, this means that in the first he would definitely have been Peleg's contemporary, outliving him by ten years, whereas in the second his death would have occurred almost two hundred years before Peleg was ever born.

The extra generation in the Septuagint is that of Cainan, occurring between Arphaxad and Salah. Along with the increase in number of years within the generations themselves, this amounts once again to 531 years between the Flood and

Figure 9

נֹחַ

Noah

Whether or not Peleg and Noah were contemporaries is a question dependent on chronology. According to the King James dating system, Peleg's birth and death both occurred during the prophet's lifetime. But in the Septuagint, Peleg's birth did not occur until 181 years following Noah's death.

Consequently, if the King James chronology is correct, it means that Noah most likely was involved in some way with the division of the earth and was well aware that such an event had taken place. He also might have had something to do with Peleg receiving his unusual name.

the birth of Peleg, a difference between the Septuagint and the King James Bible that results in an uncertain chronology that has significant consequences.

Peleg's and Noah's whereabouts during the time of the division are also uncertain. They might have been somewhere in Mesopotamia or farther east, beyond the Tigris River. However, even if the two men were contemporaries, there is no definite proof that Noah was living in the same area where Peleg was born.

Following the Flood, after people began to multiply and spread across the land, the main region of population appears to have been south of Mount Ararat, roughly between what is now the Persian Gulf and the Caspian Sea. From this area, there was at least a partial migration westward into Mesopotamia, the land between the two rivers.

"And the whole earth was of one language, and of one speech. And it came to pass, as they journeyed from the east, that they found a plain in the land of Shinar; and they dwelt there."[26]

Shinar was the area where Nimrod built the city of Babylon and the Tower of Babel. And since Noah would naturally disapprove of someone like Nimrod and his plans to build the tower, Noah very possibly remained in the original location, or at least somewhere outside Babylon. The same might have been true of others, including Peleg and those closely associated with the patriarchal line.

Noah and Peleg, therefore, both could have been living east of Mesopotamia, or at some place away from Babel, at the time of the earth's division. This in turn would allow for the possibility that the prophet had something to do with his third great-grandson acquiring his famous and unusual name. At the same time it would also substantiate the idea that each disapproved of Nimrod and his policies, including the construction of the notorious tower!

NIMROD AND THE

Tower

The biblical record pertaining to the Tower of Babel does not give a clear statement concerning when the tower was built, or how it related chronologically to the division of the earth. In general, however, most scholars would probably agree that the building came first, and the division second, maintaining that the word *divided* in Genesis 10:25 refers to a confusion of languages and the subsequent scattering of people. Even when the event in question is interpreted as a separation of continents or a variety of other phenomena, the order is usually the same.

But as often happens, what is popular and most accepted on an issue does not always turn out to be the truth. In regard to Nimrod and the tower, for example, the commonly accepted situation might well be in opposition to what is accurate and true. First came the division, in other words, and then as a natural consequence the construction of the Tower of Babel!

According to the historian Josephus, Nimrod said he would build a tower of refuge if it looked like God was going to destroy the world again with a flood. God had told Noah there would be no such flood and put a rainbow in the sky as a token or sign of his promise, yet Nimrod was taking no chances. Although secretly he might not have expected a problem, he nevertheless planned to respond quickly if necessary by building the highest tower the world had ever seen.

Certainly Noah and his sons trusted the Lord, and in their minds there was never any question but what the divine promise would be kept. It was just another example of people believing and having faith. Besides, there had already been one deluge, and to expect a second one so soon did not make any sense. But then came the day, theoretically, when news arrived that another flood was actually on the way!

Reports started coming in first from one direction and then another. People arriving from outside areas would tell of unusual changes in geography and a gradually increasing sea level, and although there might not have been any immediate danger, the situation was changing steadily enough to suggest there could be problems in the future. In any case, it was obvious that something different and unusual was taking place, and it might have been the main reason for Nimrod finally deciding to build the tower.

Whatever the motive, and whenever the time period, the Tower of Babel rose quickly once it was begun, or at least so goes the account by Josephus. He states that the structure "grew very high," and the work force consisted of a "multitude of hands."

If it is true, therefore, that reports of a distant flood caused Nimrod to start his building project, some important factors emerge in connection with the time of Peleg and the division of the earth. First, this kind of motive gives secondary importance to two reasons mentioned in the Bible: (1) erecting a structure that would "reach unto heaven," possibly suggesting a religious purpose, and (2) people trying to make a name for themselves by developing unity and staying together as a group.

Second, the commencement of the tower after the division had begun removes the likelihood that the division of the earth was a separation of people, linguistically and culturally or in a variety of other ways. Instead, it points to a deluge of water that might have been similar to the great Flood except that it was much more gradual in coming and resulted in a much smaller volume of water.

Third, the idea that Nimrod built the tower because of a flood threat agrees with the account given by Josephus. The implication made by the ancient historian is that the tower never would have materialized had it not been for the impending danger of a second deluge.

Finally, to say that the Tower of Babel was mainly the result of some physical disturbance or calamity relates in a significant way to the personality of Nimrod himself. It is a reminder once again that he was not a great hunter before the Lord, but instead a despotic ruler, and also that his building project was a hurried one, inspired more by fear and revenge than anything that was religious or even political.[27]

In addition, it suggests the picture of a man that is very different from the popular view. He was not an honorable person, in other words, and his construction of the great tower, far from being just a building project in a new city, might have been a deliberate act of vengeance and retaliation. Even more than this, it was a frantic race against time to create a place of safety before floodwaters arrived.

All of these factors develop not only a clearer view of Nimrod, but also the division of the earth, establishing the idea that it was a vast separation of land by water rather than any administrative action or separation of people. They also reveal the time that such a division occurred and the relationship it had to the construction of the Tower of Babel. Whereas previously the division has often been placed after the tower, for example, instead of before, the possibility now is that the situation was just the reverse, and whatever it was that took place in those days was in direct response to the threat of an incoming flood!

A RAINBOW IN THE
Sky

On one occasion following the great Flood, God spoke to Noah and his three sons and promised them there would never be another deluge that would kill all mankind. He further stated that the earth itself would be protected.

"And I will establish my covenant with you," he told them. "Neither shall all flesh be cut off anymore by the waters of a flood; neither shall there any more be a flood to destroy the earth."

After that, he gave them a sign that what he said was true, namely the rainbow in the sky. Whenever they saw it from then on, he said, it would be a reminder that the Flood was in the past and that man would never have to fear this same kind of calamity again.

The rainbow was not only a sign but a token of the covenant as well. It was the Lord's way of putting a seal upon his promise, one that held him bound even though he was a ruler over the universe. It is significant also that he made a similar covenant as far as the earth was concerned.

"I do set my bow in the cloud," he said, "and it shall be for a token of a covenant between me and the earth."[28]

In Noah's mind, therefore, the Flood was over. It was finished. God might bring about future disasters in response to the waywardness of mankind, but at least there would never again be a devastating flood.

And yet it would only be natural for Noah to wonder about various news reports, if they actually did occur, concerning another approaching deluge. Especially as the news kept coming in, telling of an increasing sea level, he might have thought of the rainbow many times and continually gone over in his mind what the Lord had said. In the back of his mind also would be the recollection of the first flood. Nothing could ever take that away. And then when he saw the same kind of thing happening again, although much slower this time, he definitely would wonder what was taking place.

What Noah did not know, however, if all of these things indeed did trouble him, was that the deluge on the horizon was much different from the former one, despite the similarities. This was not a flood of retribution, for one thing, but one whose main purpose was to transform land surfaces.

It was also significantly different in another way. The first flood, accompanied by heavy rainfall, had taken five months to reach its highest level, but the second would possibly be much longer. In fact, the deluge that caused the division of the earth during Peleg's time might actually have continued for several years, producing an extensive change in topography as water moved in from somewhere in the north.

And as new areas of water developed, encroaching upon what earlier had been one gigantic section of land, people would naturally speculate and worry, even Noah to some degree. With each new report telling of an increase in sea level, it would not take long for emotional levels to approach a stage of panic.

"Another flood is coming!" Nimrod would say. "Go to, let us build a tower!" Noah, on the other hand, would point to the rainbow and remind people that they should still use their faith.

At an earlier time, according to Josephus, the prophet and his sons had difficulty trying to get some of the people to descend from the mountains following the great Flood. They "were loath to come down from the higher places," he said.

Now some years later, as floodwaters again encroached upon the land, many people possibly wanted to return.

But Nimrod had a better plan, and despotic power as well, and as a result, the walls of the Tower of Babel were started and quickly began to rise!

It is not difficult to imagine some of the questions that might have gone through Noah's mind at this time. Why was another deluge on the way, for example, and what purpose would it serve? Also where would the people go if waters again did inundate the land?

In addition, there was the troublesome question of the rainbow. What was the meaning of God's promise, as well as the token of the covenant, if he was now bringing in another flood?

Fortunately, all of these questions came to naught, if indeed they ever occurred in the first place, because news allegedly arrived that a flood threat was finally over. People coming in from many different locations reported that the seas had stabilized and that water was no longer moving in upon the land. In other words, there was no longer a crisis, and the threat of a second deluge that could have destroyed the world was now a thing of the past.

Such might have been the conditions in the Middle East, therefore, and in surrounding areas during the so-called division of the earth. And although actual events and circumstances are unknown, one thing again is certain: a division historically is definitely implied, either as part of the great Flood itself or as the result of another deluge soon after. Theoretically, a tremendous volume of water, as suggested in modern scripture, came down out of the north country, emerging from underground areas and then spreading southward onto land surfaces. The result was a dramatic reconfiguration of territory that produced islands and continents as they exist in the world today.

This was also the exact time period when the man named Peleg was born, either just before the deluge or after. In view of the fact that he was designated to follow his father in the patriarchal line, however, the space of time between the division and his birth, or vice versa, could have been a considerable length of time, the special name being given to him because of his patriarchal status, rather than being given to someone else.

Moreover, depending on chronology and where he was living at the time, he might have received his name from Noah himself. The great prophet, who had presided over one deluge and now maybe two, would certainly be a likely person to bestow the honor. And in a day when people might have been commemorating the end of another flood, the time of Peleg's birth and naming would undoubtedly be an important occasion.

Also in those days there could have been not just one but two well-known sayings circulating in the land. "Even as Nimrod, the mighty hunter before the Lord," some would say in reference to the famous ruler of Babylon, and yet elsewhere, maybe further to the east away from Babel, even outside Mesopotamia, others might have been talking more about Peleg, saying that "in his days was the earth divided!"

THE ENIGMA OF A
Flood

An important question pertaining to the division of the earth is why it was such an unpublicized event. If there was indeed such a deluge, separate and distinct from the great Flood, why is it that there is no documentation of it, other than possibly a few small verses of scripture?

The actuality of the Flood a century earlier, or maybe a few hundred years before that time, is beyond question, reported not only in the Bible but in a number of other historical sources. And yet as far as the division is concerned, there is virtually nothing. It is as though a veil of secrecy had been dropped over the event from the beginning, purposely setting it apart as a subject not meant for disclosure.

Aside from single scriptures in Genesis and 1 Chronicles, along with two verses of modern scripture, there is little or no proof that a division of the earth ever took place. For more than four thousand years, it has remained an enigma. Josephus and other writers before him are all silent on anything that even resembles a second flood.

One possible reason is that ancient historians, as well as the world's population in general, may not known that the division and the Flood were both parts of the same event. Since the two deluges were so close together in time, the idea that they were separate floods never materialized.

Most people right after the great Flood might not have known that water had completely drained off, and if and when the sea level began to rise again, they were unaware that any large increase had occurred. In other words, it was not as though a tremendous deluge had again inundated the earth, but rather there was enough increase in water volume to cause a flood scare. As far as the majority of people was concerned, the situation of continents and islands already existed, and any additional flooding upon the land represented only a relatively small encroachment.

Another idea is that civilization was still young in those days in regard to total population, having started with just eight people following the Flood. Only a hundred years had elapsed since that time, according to the chronology of sources such as the King James Version of the Bible, and most people probably had not traveled to any great distance in any direction. Consequently, they would be unaware that any large flooding had occurred and that the so-called division had taken place, with the result being that very little was ever said or written about it.

It is likely that only a few people knew what was happening at the time, among whom were those involved in the naming of Peleg. As things turned out, it was that time in history when the world's population was drastically diminished due to the great Flood, and because of it the concept of a division never had a chance to take effect.

A third idea, and one that does not necessarily exclude the others, is the idea of secrecy and nondisclosure. For some reason information pertaining to the division of the earth might purposely have been relegated to obscurity until such time that a knowledge of it would be more significant. This suggests that during a later time period, the full purpose of this particular event will become more relevant, especially as far as the world in general is concerned.

And finally, there is the idea of carelessness and inadvertence. It was not because the event was underpublicized, for whatever reason, or that it was meant to be kept a secret, but only because it was taken for granted among a number of other things and somehow got lost in the shuffle.

Again it is like the Bible saying that "Enoch walked with God, and he was not, for God took him," after which the subject is dropped completely. Also in the instance of Joshua commanding the sun and moon to stand still, only a few passing comments are recorded in the biblical record, and then suddenly nothing more is said about it. This does not mean that these things were unimportant, but inadvertently or otherwise they ended up relatively lost in history. In one way or another, they became subordinate to other events and phenomena that were much less significant.

A further example is Nimrod, one of the most enigmatic figures in the Bible. Documented by only four verses in Genesis and 1 Chronicles, he is virtually unknown in each of these two records. In fact, if it were not for other sources of information, his true identity, like that of Peleg, would very likely still be a mystery.

And as far as the Tower of Babel is concerned, namely the legendary structure that Nimrod is said to have built, that also remains a mystery. The reasons for building the tower, for example, and its time period continue to be controversial subjects and are just two of the many unsolved problems pertaining to the Bible!

A MATTER OF
Chronology

An additional problem in connection with Nimrod, as well as Noah and Peleg, is one which pertains to dating systems and chronology. Again it is often not so much a question of what happened on certain occasions, as well as why, but rather the question of when. Especially in regard to Nimrod's construction of the Tower of Babel and the relationship of that event to the division of the earth, the time period involved is very indefinite.

Although several different chronologies might be used in discussing this event, the two that are often mentioned in the literature are those in the King James Version of the Bible and the Greek Version of the Old Testament known as the Septuagint. According to the first, a little more than a century occurred between the Flood in Noah's time and the birth of Peleg when the earth was divided, which was also the general time period for the commencement of the tower. But by way of the second chronology, the length of time between these two occurrences is much greater, a total of 531 years, to be exact.

This is a huge time difference, of course, and it has an important bearing not only on when the division of the earth and the building of the Tower of Babel took place, but also why the tower was built in the first place. And whereas both dating systems have their strengths and advantages, eventually it is a matter of choosing one or the other in order to develop a type of theory that is reliable and consistent.

One advantage of the Septuagint chronology is that there are less limitations as to time. Five centuries following the Flood, for example, would provide more than ample opportunity for developing a large population and constructing a tower. Yet at the same time, a huge number of people would eliminate the tower as a general place of refuge from a flood, if it had ever been meant to be used as such. The most that Nimrod could get into such a building in case of an emergency might be no more than 40,000 men, women, and children.

The King James chronology, on the other hand, is more apt to suggest that a tower was definitely necessary and was initiated because of a flood scare, even though it might pose a problem as to required manpower. In ancient times, structures like the pyramids and ziggurats were a long time in the making and usually required many thousands of workmen.

But since the theory is advanced that Nimrod started the Tower of Babel in the wake of a threatening deluge, such an idea necessitates the use of one particular chronology over the other. Consequently, in the material that follows, which refers to population increase after the Flood, as well as to the division of the earth and the construction of the Tower, the dating system used is the one found in the King James Version of the Bible.

This selection is made in spite of the fact that the system involves not only a possible manpower problem but also one of synchronizing certain events in the Bible with those in secular history, particularly the great Flood in the days of Noah. Yet in regard to the latter, it also allows for the possibility that there are extenuating circumstances that in the future might reconcile important differences and stabilize an uncertain situation.

There is an implication, for example, that certain adjustments need to be made in the King James Bible. Too many years occur before the Flood, in other words, in regard to the life spans of the patriarchs, and not enough after. Theoretically by decreasing the length of the antediluvian period and proportionately increasing the time in the generations that follow, it results in an earlier flood date, thus alleviating synchronization problems between certain biblical events and those in ancient history, in particular some pertaining to Egypt.

Also it is interesting to note that the chronology of early Egyptian dynasties does not go back in time nearly as far as it used to, even to the extent of 500 years. And according to one contemporary writer and Egyptologist, some of the dynastic periods should now be reduced even further.[29] As a consequence, this would imply that the King James date for the Flood, which presently is right in the middle of the early pyramid era, might eventually end up before Egypt began its postdiluvian history instead of after, given enough time for this type of thing to happen.

In the meantime, these different conditions do not discount the possibility, or even the preference, of other dating systems, some of which obviously might be more logical concerning certain situations. For the present, it merely means putting them on hold. At best, dating and tables of dates for anything prior to 1000 BC are still very tentative, and if there is one thing that is subject to change from time to time, it is certainly chronology!

Figure 10

Number of Years Between Generations from Adam to Abraham

(Adam lived 130 years and begat Seth, Seth lived 105 years and begat Enos, Enos lived 90 years and begat Cainan, and so forth.)

King James Version		Septuagint	
Adam	130	Adam	230
Seth	105	Seth	205
Enos	90	Enos	190
Cainan	70	Cainan	170
Mahalaleel	65	Maleleel	165
Jared	162	Jared	162
Enoch	65	Enoch	165
Methuselah	187	Mathusala	167
Lamech	182	Lamech	188
Noah	502	Noe	502
Shem	100	Sem	100
Arphaxad	35	Arphaxad	135
Salah	30	*Cainan*	130
Eber	34	Sala	130
Peleg	30	Heber	134
Reu	32	Phaleg	130
Serug	30	Ragau	132
Nahor	29	Seruch	130
Terah	70	Nachor	179
Abram	—	Tharrha	70
Total 1948		Abram	—
		Total 3414	

The main difference in the above figures is that the Septuagint version of the Bible includes an extra generation and also a much larger number of years. In addition, it suggests that the time of Adam and Eve in the Garden of Eden was about 5400 BC, whereas in the King James Version the date would be as much as 1400 years later, or in other words 4000 BC.

Yet in addition to all of this, there is still another reason for using the King James system of dating. In actuality, it might be the one important factor that dictates the use of this particular system over all others.

It has to do with a concept alluded to in the book of Revelation and outlined more specifically in modern scripture. It is the idea that the earth's history, as far as mankind's presence is concerned, is made up of six periods of one thousand years each, these to be followed eventually by a seventh period of similar length that includes the biblical Millennium.

Reference to such divisions of time constitutes an important body of information, especially in connection with religious history and prophecy, and establishes an interesting time frame as far as mankind's existence on the earth is concerned. In addition, the events pertaining to the time of Peleg are significantly involved. It is the concept of seven thousand years of history, however, that sometimes turns out to be a problem, yet at the same time a determining factor in selecting an appropriate chronology.

According to the King James dating system, the conclusion of six thousand years of recorded history would occur sometime in the vicinity of the year 2000, allowing for a certain number of years of variance due to intervening circumstances and calendar error. This would also place the beginning of mankind when Adam and Eve were in the Garden of Eden at approximately 4000 BC.

But by way of the Septuagint, for example, the beginning point for Adam would have to be set at about 5400 BC, or 4800 according to a reduced calculation, which drastically alters the idea of seven millennial periods.

In view of this, the King James dating system is again preferred over chronologies such as the Greek Septuagint as far as the Tower of Babel and the division of the earth are concerned, especially since there is the strong indication in scripture that the overall preliminary time period in human history prior to the biblical Millennium is 6000 years in duration. Also this particular system is much more likely to suggest that Nimrod's tower in Babylon was built as a place of refuge, as well as an act of vengeance toward God for devastating the world during the great Flood!

TIMETABLE OF
Events

The theory that the division in Peleg's time preceded the great Tower and was possibly the main thing that prompted its construction is a controversial idea. Although it is in sharp contrast with certain other views, and also unorthodox in its nature, it is nevertheless a concept that might be closest to the truth.

An important premise, once again, is that the event in question pertaining to the division does not refer to a separation or scattering of people at the time the languages were confounded. Instead it pertains to a period of history approximately one hundred years after the Flood, according to the King James chronology, when the land surface of the earth was divided into islands and continents. This event occurred when the last of three great deluges swept down out of the north country. Once this type of premise is accepted, certain observations can then be made.

1) Out of several possible motives for building the Tower of Babel, the most logical could have been the threat of a devastating flood. There is a scriptural implication that a mammoth deluge took place during the days of Peleg, and since Peleg's time was also the general time period of Nimrod's tower, it follows that the two were in some way connected. In view of this, the other motives lose much of their significance, namely

the idea that people were trying to build a tower that would reach to heaven and at the same time stay together and make a name for themselves.

The fact that the latter two reasons are the only ones mentioned in the Bible does not preclude the first one. Rather it would appear that something very important has been left out of the biblical record! Just as very little is said about Nimrod as a person, much is also missing as to why he built the tower, and also when.

2) If the commencement of the tower is placed after the division of the earth instead of before it, circumstances surrounding the principal figure involved are put into a more meaningful perspective. Even during the later period, for example, Nimrod might not have had much time to be born, grow up, and ascend to a position of power in the government prior to the tower being built. In the earlier period, the time problem would have been especially difficult.

All of this would depend, of course, on when Nimrod was born. If it were at the same time as his second cousin Salah, it would place his birth at about thirty-seven years after the Flood. However, in the biblical record, five brothers are mentioned before him, which might suggest that he was born a number of years later. In any case, his age after the division of the earth, compared to what it would have been before, would give him that much more time to become the ruler of Babylon.

In contrast, by way of the Septuagint chronology, the time between the Flood and Salah's birth is 137 years instead of 37, a difference that would reduce or eliminate any time problem.

3) Theoretically, it would take a lot of people many years to build the Tower of Babel, even partially up to the time that construction was interrupted during the confusion of tongues. By comparison, one hundred thousand workers allegedly spent twenty years in building the Great Pyramid of Gizeh, and the situation pertaining to the famous ziggurats in Mesopotamia, as well as the tower, in some ways might not have been much different.

Consequently, to put the tower before the earth's division instead of after would be trying to put too much activity into a small amount of time. It would also create a problem of not having enough people to do what the account in the Bible requires.

Only eight individuals, for example, took part in initiating the repopulation of the earth following the great Flood, and considering the age of Noah and his wife, there might have been just six. This means that during the first one hundred years, up to the time of Peleg and the division, there were definite limitations as to what could be done. Even with people marrying young and having extremely large families, the multiplication factor would present a problem.

At most, the new world population after three generations probably did not exceed 1300 people if Noah's three sons were the only ones having children, or 1700 if Noah himself were involved. The situation is further complicated by the fact that a large percentage of these numbers would be of a very young age. And as far as the construction of the Tower of Babel is concerned, some of the total population might not even have been available for the work force, never having left the original area east of Mesopotamia.

What this amounts to, therefore, is definitely a time problem, one that implies that the tower would have had to be started after the earth was divided and not before. It means that whatever it was that happened at that time was controlled largely by a set of numbers. Population figures, in other words, would have had to match up with the events taking place, or there would have been no consistency or reality. It is this last observation that is crucial in developing a plausible theory pertaining to the division of the earth and at the same time establishing an accurate timetable of events!

The Problem of
Numbers

Repopulating the earth following the Flood was undoubtedly very slow at first, with maybe forty or fifty people existing after twenty years. At the end of another twenty it might have been little more than two hundred, depending on the number of couples with families, how early they began having children, and also how often.

Actually it was not until children began coming from the third generation after the deluge that any significant increase occurred. By then more than half a century had gone by, and according to one optimistic view, construction of the Tower of Babel was almost ready to begin.

In regard to the tower, however, it obviously was not the right time. Considering the number of people involved, there was far from enough manpower to build it. Besides, Nimrod was possibly still a child, or maybe not even born yet.

It is easy to overlook how slowly population increases when it has to start from a low number. The first two generations after the Flood, in fact, were mainly a preparatory phase in which children grew up, got married, and finally began having families. Because of this, placing the Tower of Babel anywhere within the first eighty years would be entirely out of the question.

At the same time, it is not surprising to find that things began happening very quickly during the latter part of the century. Not only was there a rapid increase in population, but Nimrod had the necessary time to rise to a position of authority that eventually started him thinking about building a place of refuge, if and when conditions required it. But whatever the circumstances might have been, the existing number of people was definitely a crucial factor!

The situation is also related to the man named Peleg and whether he was born before the division of the earth or after it. According to the King James chronology, his birth took place 101 years following the Flood, which means that if it occurred before the division, there would be at least a century for population increase prior to the building of the tower, a span of time that was definitely needed. If the birth occurred after the earth was divided, however, it would suggest that the tower was possibly already underway.

All of this depends upon the theory, of course, that the conditions pertaining to the division were regarded as a flood threat and were the primary reason for the tower's construction.

The logical time for Peleg to be born would have been soon after the earth was divided so that he could be named for something that had already happened. But in this situation, there might be a population problem of not having enough adult members to provide a necessary work force.

On the other hand, if Peleg was born before the division, possibly even several years, it would put more time between him and the building of the tower and consequently provide additional years for population growth. In this case, an original name given to him might have been changed in order to commemorate an important event that could have taken place anywhere from 100 to 120 years following the Flood.

It is amazing what an additional generation would amount to in terms of population growth during those twenty years. The number of people, for example, could have increased from 35,000 to as many as 150,000. And that would be in connection with Shem, Ham, and Japheth only, not including Noah. This means that during an extra generation, when it actually did occur, there might not have been so much the problem of finding enough people to build the Tower of Babel, but instead finding room for everyone once it was finished!

A NEW
Population

Out of several different methods of theorizing population growth, one possibility is to assign five generations to a century. This includes an extremely energetic system of multiplication, and one which at first glance might seem unreasonable, yet it is nevertheless one that is suggested by the King James chronology. In other words, at least a certain number of people would be necessary to account for what happened during the first one hundred years after the Flood, according to the biblical account, and in regard to this kind of situation, the system in question might be described as follows.

(1) An average marriage would take place at age twenty for a male and eighteen for a female. (2) Births in a family would occur every two years. (3) Children would marry within their own group or intermarry with members of another family. (4) Each generation would comprise twenty years.

Of course, this type of arrangement is not without difficulties. Possibly the main problem has to do with the idea of five generations per one hundred years, which is not easily reconciled with the Bible. During the first century following the Flood, for example, only three people were born into the patriarchal line, those being Arphaxad, Salah, and Eber, and these men had their first recorded children when they were thirty-five, thirty, and thirty-four years old, respectively. Obviously

this at first implies that there might have been three generations to a century instead of four or five.

And yet the system that contains five and produces a larger
population is one that people needed in those days if they were
to keep up with what was eventually recorded in history and to
act out the account recorded in the eleventh chapter of Genesis,
namely building the city of Babylon and starting the Tower of
Babel. Also the generation sequence of Arphaxad, Salah, and
Eber does not necessarily establish a representative number of
generations or frequency of birth during this 100-year period.
The pattern of population increase undoubtedly was more
varied and complex.

By way of a five-generation arrangement, therefore, population growth in the Mesopotamian area by the end of sixty
years would have reached a fairly significant stage, although
probably no more than 1,300 people, certainly not enough to
start building a tower. At the conclusion of eighty years, the
total would have been much higher, possibly around 7,000 if
Noah's sons were the only ones involved, yet still not enough
for a mammoth building project, even if conducted under
emergency conditions.

But by the end of the first century, as many as 36,000
people or more could have been living in Mesopotamia, in
the valley itself as well as in other places further east. And if
Noah himself was still having children, the total would have
been considerably more. Consequently, this type of population
increase during the five generations following the great Flood
might now be viewed as creating a plausible work force.

All of these totals contain optimistic figures, however,
since they make no allowance for such variables as fatal disease and infant mortality. In addition, there is always the
negative aspect of conjecture, along with speculation, as to
what might have happened. Yet at the same time, there is a
positive assertion that things during the first century after
the Flood definitely could have taken place according to the
conditions and chronology in one particular set of scripture.

Flaws in reasoning and calculation, if and when they do exist, do not significantly alter an original intent and purpose, which is to show that circumstances during this time period were pretty much as they are set forth in the King James Version of the Bible.

Finally one more factor is present that further complicates things. It pertains to the last part of the century where the number of people suddenly showed a tremendous increase. Those born in the concluding twenty years, for example, mostly Noah's great-grandchildren at several different generation levels, amounted to more than 80 percent of the total population. In general this means that 2,900 adult couples produced 29,000 children in those days, and one-half of these were age ten and under!

These last figures suggest something very remarkable and unexpected! And that is that Nimrod's work force might have comprised not only men and women but a large number of children as well. This in turn reestablishes the idea that a serious emergency existed and that at least one hundred years of population increase following the great Flood were needed in order to have the kind of work force necessary to start building the Tower of Babel!

Figure 11

Population Diagram

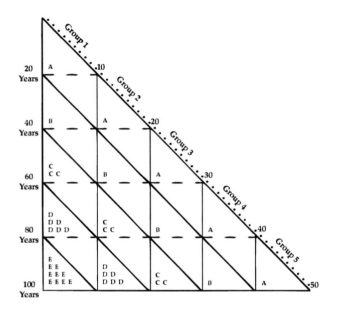

The dots at the top of the diagram graphically represent the fifty children born to Shem, one of the sons of Noah, over a span of 100 years following the Flood. The letters within the five 20-year periods show how these children and their posterity multiplied. (See Figures 12 and 13.)

In addition, it is theorized that Ham and Japheth, Noah's other two sons, also had an average of 50 children each during the first century. Consequently, their multiplication process would be like the one pertaining to Shem. And if Noah himself was still having children, his situation would be the same except on a more limited basis.

Figure 12a

Population Growth After the Flood

Shem, Ham, and Japheth, and possibly Noah himself repopulated the earth following the Flood. The way in which the population might have developed over the first one hundred years can be seen by looking at one of Noah's sons.

Shem, for example, possibly had 50 children during that time, based on a birth rate of one child every two years. These children along with their posterity are represented as follows.

		Number of Years				
Children		0–20	20–40	40–60	60–80	80–100
1st 10	Group 1	A	B	C	D	E
				CC	DD	EE
					DDD	EEE
						EEEE
2nd 10	Group 2		A	B	C	D
					CC	DD
						DDD
3rd 10	Group 3			A	B	C
						CC
4th 10	Group 4				A	B
5th 10	Group 5					A

In Group 1 Shem had 10 children (1-A). As they matured and reached a marriageable age of eighteen or twenty, they separated into five couples and had 10 children each, or a total of 50 (Shem's 1st set of grandchildren) (1-B). These 50 children eventually divided into 25 couples, each of whom also had 10 children, amounting to a total of 250. (Shem's 1st set of great-grandchildren) (1C).

Figure 12b (continued from 12a)

They in turn separated into 125 couples and had 1,250 children (Shem's 1st set of 2nd great-grandchildren) (1-D). These then divided into 625 couples and had 6,250 children (Shem's 1st set of 3rd great-grandchildren) (1-E).

Going back in time, Shem's first 10 children, after having 50 offspring, then went on to have 50 more (Shem's 2nd set of grandchildren (1-CC). These eventually separated into 25 couples and had 250 children (Shem's 2nd set of great-grandchildren) (1-DD). They then divided into 125 couples and had 1,250 children (Shem's 2nd set of 2nd great-grandchildren) (1-EE).

Reverting again in time, Shem's first 10 children again had 50 additional offspring (Shem's 3rd set of grandchildren) (1-DDD). These separated into 25 couples and had 250 children of their own (Shem's 3rd set of great-grandchildren) (1-EEE). And finally this same group, after 150 children during the first eighty years after the Flood, had 50 more (Shem's 4th set of grandchildren) (1-EEEE).

In Group 1, therefore, the multiplication process can be viewed in relation to Shem's first ten children during a period of 100 years. In Group 2 it is the same kind of process except that Shem's second ten children are the ones that are involved, and the time period is only 80 years, and so forth, with the other three groups continuing in the same way down to the end of the century.

(Note: In order to reach a total population figure for the first one hundred years, the above process is also applied to Noah's other sons, and possibly at least to some degree to Noah himself.)

Figure 13a

First Century Statistics

Group 1 (Shem)

1-A	1–20 years	1st set of children	10
B	20–40	1st g-children	50
C	40–60	1st gg-children	250
D	60–80	1st 2gg-children	1,250
E	80–100	1st 3gg-children	6,250
			7,810
1-CC	40–60 years	2nd g-children	50
DD	60–80	2nd gg-children	250
EE	80–100	2nd 2gg-children	1,250
			1,550
1-DDD	60–80 years	3rd g-children	50
EEE	80–100	3rd gg-children	250
			300
1-EEEE	80–100 years	4th g-children	50
			50
		Total	**9,710**

Group 2 (Shem)

2-A	20–40 years	2nd set of children	10
B	40–60	5th g-children	50
C	60–80	4th gg-children	250
D	80–100	3rd 2gg-children	1,250
			1,560
2-CC	60–80	6th g-children	50
DD	80–100	5th g-children	250
			300
2-DDD	80–100	7th g-children	50
			50
		Total	**1,910**

Figure 13b (continued from 13a)

First Century Statistics

Group 3 (Shem)

3-A	40–60 years	3rd set of children	10
B	60–80	8th g-children	50
C	80–100	6th gg-children	250
			310
3-CC	80–100 years	9th g-children	50
			360

Group 4 (Shem)

4-A	60–80 years	4th set of children	10
B	80–100 years	10th g-children	50
			60

Group 5 (Shem)

5-A	80–100 years	5th set of children	10
			10
		Total	12,050

Summary of First 100 Years

12,050		
x3		
36,150	Posterity of Shem, Ham, and Japheth	
+8	Original 8 People on the Ark	
36,158	Total Population	

12,050		
x4		
48,200	Posterity of the 3 Sons and Noah	
+8	Original 8 People on the Ark	
48,208	Toal Population	

It is questionable whether Noah had more children after the Flood. If not, the population at the end of the first century might have been approximately 36,158. If Noah did have children, however, theoretically at the same rate as his sons, which is unlikely, it could have amounted to a total such as 48,208.

A Place of

Refuge

Besides the problem of not enough people to build a tower, there is also the possibility once again that in another way there might have been too many. In other words, because of a limited amount of space, some of those looking for safety in such a structure might have been unable to find it.

On the one hand, it was a matter of locating the necessary workers who could quickly erect a building, while on the other hand, it was providing enough room for them and also their families once the building was finished. Obviously, the factor of seating capacity, or living capacity, was important.

Given the possibility that more than 35,000 people were living in Babylon and surrounding areas at the time, it might appear unreasonable at first that all of them could find refuge in a single structure, at an elevation high enough to avoid rising floodwaters. There would be too many occupants for the amount of space available. Yet a modern example, that of a large stadium that seats a comparable number of spectators, gives a certain amount of credence to the idea of a tower.

It might be argued that if such a stadium could be built today in one or two years, a similar edifice in earlier times could have been erected in three or four. It would have looked much different, of course, varying in design and rising higher above the ground, but it could have still provided a temporary place of refuge when completed, and furnished a certain degree of safety.[30]

Many such structures existed in the ancient world. The design of a Mesopotamian ziggurat, in fact, although smaller in size, gives a general idea of how the Tower of Babel might have looked if completed. The latter undoubtedly had a higher elevation, especially if flood danger was a motivating factor, and there was probably considerable inner space in addition to extra levels and terraces. But with the right kind of architecture, it is conceivable that such a building could accommodate up to 35,000 people, a large number of whom would be small children.

A typical artists's conception of the ancient tower shows a tall, slender construction with a spiraling path or staircase. Inhabitants are seen standing on the outer edges of the building or looking out through portals and windows. A more plausible situation, however, and one that is much more reconcilable with an extensive population, might be the kind that shows a building with platforms, large flat areas where several thousand people could assemble together at one time. This is the kind of structure that is more likely to gain credibility.

Finally, in addition to all of the speculation, and aside from any arguments pertaining to a tower, there is the suggestion that there might have been a better way, a more practical method of dealing with the problem. If Nimrod was really concerned about another flood, for example, why did he ignore the mountains, which were not too far to the east, as a place of safety? Certainly they would have afforded a greater elevation than any structure he could hope to build.

Yet in answer to such a question, Nimrod himself might have given the following reasons: (1) It was important not just to build a tower for security but to continue the plans for building a city. (2) The tower was also a good way of unifying the people and keeping them under control. (3) In addition, such a building could serve a dual purpose, not only providing

Figure 14

Mesopotamian Ziggurat

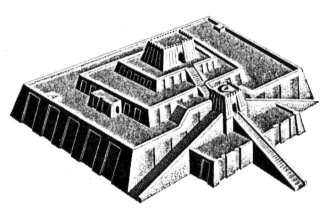

Instead of the Tower of Babel being a tall, slender structure with a spiraling stairway, as is often depicted in art, it was possibly more rectangular in appearance, consisting of a series of terraces and looking much like a Sumerian or Babylonian ziggurat. It probably had a greater height than such buildings, with several additional levels, but in style of architecture it might have been basically the same.

protection from a potential flood, but at the same time serving as a religious edifice. (4) The world in those days needed innovation and leadership, and building the tower was one way of showing it.

Nimrod's advice to his people, according to Josephus, was to trust in their own ingenuity and rely upon their industry and resourcefulness. Nothing was more important, he said, than to have confidence in themselves, knowing they could do anything if they worked hard enough and put their minds to it.

Theoretically, it definitely looked like a second flood was on the way, judging from outside reports, yet it was slower than the first, and there was still time to do something about it. There was also a possibility that the new deluge would be much less severe this time, making the building of boats or any retreat to the mountains unnecessary if everyone was willing to cooperate and help build the tower. It was a matter of people responding to a critical situation and then going to work.

And very possibly that is exactly what happened! If the words of Josephus can be relied upon, at least to a certain extent, it means that a "multitude of hands" was immediately employed in a tremendous building project, one that caused a huge and strange form to rise quickly above the land. It was the type of thing no one had ever seen before, and even the workers, which might have included hundreds of women and children, were surprised at how fast the building grew.

Indeed this was the Tower of Babel, the future showplace of the rising city of Babylon and the most notorious edifice in the ancient world. This was Nimrod's folly, a giant enterprise destined for failure from the beginning and soon to be interrupted not by a menacing flood in the distance but by another event commenced by God himself, the famous confusion of tongues and subsequent scattering of people. Yet more than anything else the building was the project of a very misguided man, a foolish man's idea that lacked prudence and foresight, as well as reason and good sense, and as a consequence turned out to be a costly and unprofitable undertaking.

The presumption that even a small number of people could survive a future deluge without such things as a huge food supply and proper equipment is unreasonable. And then to suggest that a tower would benefit the entire population of Babylon is further without reason. The likelihood once again is that Nimrod himself did not actually believe that another flood was coming but was using mounting news reports to promote his own purposes. Certainly there are many possibilities as to what took place, but if Josephus was correct when he said Nimrod planned to build a tower in reaction to an alarming situation, the idea that he built it in spite of impractical conditions and circumstances probably has some credibility.

In any case, at least according to theory, the Tower of Babel was an impressive monument to the gigantic division of the earth then in progress, a sign or symbol, as it were, of the massive deluge of water heading toward Mesopotamia and like the historic changing of languages soon to occur also an act of deity and the result of a divine command!

A DIVINE

Edict

In regard to the possibility that there were three large deluges in history, one of the things they all appear to have in common is that each was the result of a divine edict. It is the idea that they were not just physical phenomena or unusual upheavals of nature, but spiritual occurrences as well, events initiated by deity that significantly affected the affairs of mankind.

Such a command, which occurred on the third day of Creation, was what caused the original floodwaters to subside. "Let the waters under heaven be gathered together unto one place," God said, "and let the dry land appear."[31] Things did not just happen in a way that was scientific or evolutionary but instead were all part of a divine plan and timetable. And if an order was given for the first deluge to end, it is logical that one occurred earlier that caused it to begin.

The same is true of the great Flood in the time of Noah. Although it is not recorded that there were any divine commands, two are nevertheless implied, one in a forewarning at the beginning of the flood and the other in a passage of wind toward the end.

"For yet seven days, and I will cause it to rain upon the earth forty days and forty nights," the Lord said, "and every living substance that I have made will I destroy from off the face of the earth." And then a few months later, according to the book of Genesis, he "made a wind to pass over the earth, and the waters assuaged."[32] At this time the decree once again was given to gather the oceans together and cause dry land to appear.

It was similar, on a smaller scale, to the time that Jesus rebuked the wind and water and caused a great calm to come upon the Sea of Galilee. His disciples were very impressed that day, even fearful, as they reflected on what had happened. "What manner of man is this!" they exclaimed. "For he commandeth even the winds and water, and they obey him."[33]

The Galilean incident was just a small thing in comparison with the day of Creation and the Flood, but it is a reminder that the God of the universe is in complete control of the elements. Most of the time he lets things take a natural course, but on occasion, where much is at stake as far as mankind in concerned, he intercedes and alters the situation dramatically with a divine command. It is as though he measures the waters in the hollow of his hand, as Isaiah said, and then metes out the appropriate action.

This same kind of power is mentioned in the book of Proverbs where it says that God "gave to the sea his decree, that the waters should not pass his commandment."[34] Giant floods come and go, in other words, not incidentally or inadvertently but according to a predetermined plan and timetable. And in no case is this more evident than in the third and final deluge.

In the tenth chapter of Genesis, when the Bible states that in Peleg's days the earth was divided, it is tantamount to saying that the Lord issued the decree for another flood, one that divided the earth's surface with water and created islands and continents.

This particular event was then scheduled to reverse itself more than four millennia later, the water going back to where it came from in the north and the earth returning to its original condition. It is this final occurrence, set for sometime in the latter days, that is described in two small verses of modern scripture in the record known as the Doctrine and Covenants.

"He shall command the great deep," the text says, referring to the Lord's edict, "and it shall be driven back into the north countries, and the islands shall become one land; and the land of Jerusalem and the land of Zion shall be turned back into their own place, and the earth shall be like as it was in the days before it was divided."[35] The record then goes on to describe other conditions pertaining to the last days.

This will then be the end of the giant deluges and the final time that the seas and oceans will be gathered together. No more will the earth be divided by way of water. The land surface of the globe will again become much like Pangaea of old, and everything will be as it was in the beginning, at which time the earth will be renewed and restored to a paradisiacal glory!

THE LAW OF
Restoration

An important subject related to the division of the earth, and especially to the final return of floodwaters, is one that might be referred to as the Law of Restoration. Common and familiar in some ways yet relatively unknown in others, it constitutes a significant concept and comprises several different parts or aspects.

1) One part of the law, as it pertains to human beings, states that after people die, they will eventually be resurrected, at which time they are to be restored to a proper frame and order. By way of this process, a perfected body will be restored to its spirit, in other words, and the spirit to the body, never again to be separated.

People at this time will be exempt from disease, death, and physical infirmities. Every part and function of the body, as well as conditions such as missing limbs, blindness, different kinds of deformity, and retardation will be perfected, everything assuming an ideal and natural state.

2) In another sense, involving a more abstract and spiritual part of the law, each person will also be rewarded according to the kind of life he or she has lived. There will be a restorative action in which someone who has led a good life will be restored to that which is good, while those who deliberately choose to do otherwise will be restored to the opposite. All of

this is a vital part of the Law of Restoration, and if it were any other way, the demands of justice could not be fulfilled.

3) These physical and spiritual events are very important, each occurring in connection with a future resurrection, but there is also a third aspect of the law, said to be now in progress. It is mentioned briefly in the New Testament where the Apostle Peter refers to a type of restitution.

"And he shall send Jesus Christ, which before was preached unto you," he says, referring to the Lord's Second Coming, "whom the heaven must receive until the restitution of all things, which God hath spoken by the mouth of all his holy prophets since the world began."[36]

This restitution, according to the interpretation of the Law of Restoration, means that many things pertaining to the gospel of Jesus Christ that have been discontinued or lost down through the ages are to be brought back again sometime during the latter days. All of the religious principles and ordinances that were introduced and practiced during the times of Adam, Enoch, Noah, Abraham, and Moses, as well as during Christ's ministry, are at one time or another to be restored to the earth in their fulness.

This belief, however, is not widely recognized and accepted. Most people, in fact, would probably class it more as theory than anything else, regarding it as only one among many religious philosophies. The truth of it as far as they are concerned is yet to be established. But in the meantime, despite any skepticism or doubt, it continues to be an interesting concept and in the field of religion stands as a very detailed and explanatory doctrine.

4) A fourth part of the Law of Restoration pertains to the so-called gathering of the House of Israel, also allegedly taking place at the present time. It states that the different Israelite tribes that have been scattered down through the centuries, or rather their descendants, are to be gathered again in the last days and eventually restored to the lands of their inheritance. People in this particular group and lineage, including those

who are adopted into it, will be an important motivating force and influence as the world nears the time for entering the Millennium.

5) In conclusion, there is still another part of this unusual law, one that is directly associated with the days of Peleg and the geographical division of the earth. It involves the idea that the earth is not only an astronomical and geological entity but a living organism that has certain characteristics analogous to those of a human being.

In this relation, it is said to have a spiritual nature along with one that is physical. Consequently, it can be viewed as much more than just a material object in the universe. As the spirit and body of an individual constitute the soul of man, for example, so might the combined spiritual and temporal parts of the planet be regarded as the soul of the earth.

This means that the earth, following its creation or birth, eventually entered a type of existence that in some ways is like that of a human being. It then began a progression through a series of stages that are spiritual as well as physical. From a religious viewpoint, this included a baptism by water at the time of the great Flood, and at a future date during a time period referred to as the end of the world, there will also be a baptism by fire. These two occurrences, in addition to being physical catastrophes, might also be considered types of religious ordinances.

It is in connection with a final baptism of fire that the earth will be cleansed and restored to a previous glory, following a vast series of earthquakes effecting transformation and change. Conditions once more will be like those that existed in the Garden of Eden, with many valleys being transformed and many hills and mountains broken down. It will be the same type of situation as described by the prophet Isaiah when he said that "every valley shall be exalted, and every mountain and hill shall be made low: and the crooked shall be made straight, and the rough places plain."[37]

During those days the world will experience a remarkable transformation. Everything on the surface of the planet will be made new. The land of Jerusalem in Palestine and the land of Zion in America "shall be turned back into their own place, and the earth shall be like as it was in the days before it was divided."[38] Then will come the thousand years of history known as the Millennium, after which the earth itself will eventually die and be resurrected. All of this represents an important and miraculous sequence of events, part of a mortal probation, as it were, that the earth will accomplish in order to obtain its own type of salvation and exaltation.

At the beginning of the Millennium, however, after partially filling the measure of its creation, the planet earth will enter a new and final stage of progression. At that time, prior to a death and resurrection, it will be restored to a more perfect and original condition and will be rewarded according to the principles and concepts in the Law of Restoration.

This unusual view of the earth, based on both faith and intellect, is itself a type of miracle. It is something very different from geological and astronomical explanations and in some ways opposite. And yet at the same time, it is the unorthodox aspect of the idea that gives it credibility when viewed within the context of biblical and Christian theology. It is also a concept providing valuable insight concerning the days of Peleg, as well as the mammoth deluges that have played such an important part in the world's history!

PELEG IN
Perspective

Another interesting theory that places attention on
Peleg is that the division of the earth was not a deluge or any
other upheaval of nature but rather a dividing point between
a longer and shorter human life span. It was a time when the
age of a man suddenly showed a dramatic decrease. Such a
phenomenon had actually begun with Shem, one of the sons of
Noah, and continued during the three generations after him,
but it was in Peleg's time that another significant and notice-
able change took place.

Those who espouse this kind of theory maintain that
the division was a period of time that separated an older
group of mankind from one that is younger, people on one
side of the line living 400 years or more and those on the
other closer to 200 or fewer. Although this view might have
certain problems and inconsistencies, it does draw attention to an important fact: Peleg lived a relatively short life.
His death, in fact, according to the King James chronology,
occurred even before that of Noah, who was more than 700
years older.

Not only would this put Peleg's death before that of his
third great-grandfather but also before the four patriarchs
who followed. His father, grandfather, and two others all died
at a later time. Because of this, it is no wonder that some have

regarded Peleg's life span as a significant dividing point.

This particular division, however, is still not the one recorded in the tenth chapter of Genesis where a much more important meaning was intended. At the time the earth was divided, in other words, it was not a social or cultural phenomenon that took place but one that was entirely physical and geographical. A tremendous transformation in nature occurred in which much of the earth's surface underwent a remarkable change, not by way of geological forces necessarily such as rising and sinking terrain, although some of this might have been present, but mainly as the result of a huge influx of floodwater. It was one of world history's most dramatic events, and as things turned out, Peleg became its namesake!

This does not imply any great significance for Peleg, only that he happened to be born at the right time and in the right place. Actually it would appear that he himself, as far as the world is concerned, could have been relatively unimportant. His name might be regarded as well known and famous, but as an individual he lies mostly in obscurity.

Yet at the same time, the question again needs to be asked: Who is it that the Bible is talking about when it refers to the one born at the time of the division? Exactly who was the man named Peleg?

Was he mainly an unknown figure except for his membership in a prestigious family, and could another just as well have been mentioned in his place had he been born under the same circumstances? Was it only because of a flood that he acquired any extra attention at all?

Or like Enoch before him, or even Nimrod in his own way, is it possible that he was much more significant as an individual than the scriptural text would indicate? Like the monumental event with which he is associated, could he also have been inadvertently or purposely bypassed in history and consequently lost by the wayside?

Obviously, Peleg is an example once again of a person or

event shrouded in mystery because of a brief reference in scripture. And only when a more complete account is written concerning him and his time period will his true identity as a man finally become known!

Purpose of a
Deluge

Two important questions that arise in connection with the days of Peleg is why there was a large influx of water at this particular time in history, so close to the great Flood, and what purpose did it serve other than causing a division of the earth into islands and continents.

To begin with, whatever the purpose might have been, it would seem that it could have been taken care of at the end of the Flood itself that had occurred only a hundred years before, or according to a different chronology several centuries earlier. Instead of all of the floodwater draining off in five or five and a half months, as suggested in the book of Genesis, a lesser amount might have receded so that the earth ended up as it did during Peleg's time, with a new configuration of land and the correct amount of sea and ocean. At least this would have brought the number of floods down to two rather than three and avoided the question of why an extra flood occurred.

Although this idea is a definite possibility, things might not have happened that way. No clues are mentioned in the Bible as to why or why not, but there are good reasons for rejecting such a theory, even though it would simplify things. There are also no definite clues given as to why the earth was divided in the first place.

Figure 15
The Number of Deluges

It is possible that the division of the earth was not a separate deluge by itself but merely the tail end, so to speak, of the great Flood in the days of Noah. In other words, when the Flood was over, the waters did not entirely subside but stopped at a point during Peleg's time that provided the network of islands and continents as they exist today.

Certainly this explanation would simplify things, such as avoiding the question as to why two large deluges were so close to one another. But the most logical solution is not always correct, and in connection with the event pertaining to Peleg, this might very well be true.

There are at least three reasons, for example, why the division was one of three giant floods, separate and distinct from the other two.

1) The wording in the biblical text suggests that this particular deluge occurred abruptly and independently. It was not merely the culmination of the great Flood. Otherwise, the text might have stated that during the days of Peleg, "the earth was finally divided" or that "the division of land became complete."

2) If the division was the point at which the Flood completely came to an end, establishing the system of present-day islands and continents, the question arises as to how people in those days knew that such a point had been reached. The scriptural text, once again, implies a more distinct and observable event.

3) The naming of Peleg also suggests a separate occurrence. It strongly intimates that when he was born, something remarkable took place. The division of the earth, in other words, was not just a situation in which geography changed gradually over a considerable period of time and then stopped at a point unknown to most people, but an event that happened separately and attracted a great deal of interest and attention. It was not a catastrophe like the deluge in the time of Noah, yet very possibly a flood scare nevertheless, one which might have caused considerable anxiety and alarm.

An important purpose of the division, however, was evidently in one way or another related to the building of the Tower of Babel. In fact, because of the biblical language involved, many believe that the confounding of tongues and the wide dispersion of people as recorded in the book of Genesis were exactly what the Bible was talking about when it said the earth was divided.

"These are the families of the sons of Noah, after their generations, in their nations: and by these were the nations divided in the earth after the flood."[39]

The confusion arises in the fact that there were actually two types of division: a dividing of the nations and also a dividing of the earth, both taking place at about the same time. Each was related in its own way to the Tower of Babel, yet the two were definitely different occurrences.

Concerning the division of nations, the Bible is very explicit. "So the Lord scattered them abroad from thence upon the face of all the earth: and they left off to build the city. Therefore is the name of it called Babel; because the Lord did there confound the language of all the earth."[40]

But again this is not to be confused with the division of the earth itself that resulted in the present-day geography of islands and continents, even though the two events are closely related.

An important reason for the earth being divided during the days of Peleg, in fact, was allegedly to set the stage for an extensive division of population. Some of the people were to be scattered into adjacent land areas, but others were destined to cross the oceans and inhabit isles of the sea. And in order for the latter to occur, there needed to be a much greater amount of water.

The intent was not only to section off various parts of the earth's land surface in preparation for future migrations, but at the same time keep certain people isolated from the rest of the world, for whatever reason. This was especially true of people known as the Jaredites, who according to modern scripture left the Tower of Babel during the confusion of tongues and began a long journey, possibly toward the east and across the Indian and Pacific Oceans, to establish a large civilization on the American continent.

The account of the Jaredites, which begins about 2200 BC, or a few centuries earlier by way of a different chronology, suggests that they were one of the earliest migrations to leave the vicinity of the tower. It also implies that at that time, the division of the earth had already taken place, since seas and oceans existed where previously there had been mainly land.

In the same account of modern scripture, reference is made not only to the Jaredites but to other groups who later made similar voyages. One writer, for example, representing a party that also went to the American continent, stated that the Lord had made the ocean their path and, as he put it, had led them to a destination that was on an isle of the sea.

"But great are the promises of the Lord," he said, "unto them who are upon the isles of the sea; wherefore as it says isles, there must needs be more than this, and they are inhabited also by our brethren."[41]

The third deluge during the time of Peleg, therefore, was a gigantic enterprise that opened the way for one migration after another to various parts of the world. It was one of the Lord's ways of scattering the nations and in some instances keeping them separate from one another in a variety of geographical locations. Beginning with the Jaredites at the time of the Tower of Babel and during different time periods that followed, the earth's waterways became literal pathways for a wide dispersion of people.

Yet as to why a third deluge in close proximity to a second was necessary to accomplish this, if indeed such an event did occur, no definite answer is given. There is nothing in secular or religious discussions that even comes close to such an idea. In fact, if it were not for a certain concept in modern scripture representing an unorthodox view of the earth and its destiny, the question likely would still lack any kind of solution.

But there is a theory and a possible answer, one that relates to the concept of a universal flood during the time of Noah and the ark. It is the idea that the great Flood in those days was not just a partial inundation of the earth but one that covered its entire surface. It was the earth's baptism, so to speak, a complete immersion in water comparable to a religious sacrament or ordinance, at which time the planet returned to the way it was in the beginning. In this way, having gone through a complete cycle, the earth was cleansed and ready to enter a new phase of existence, including the division of land into islands and continents. One flood was necessary, in other words, before another could begin.

This means that two deluges, very similar in some ways, occurred within a relatively brief time of one another, following which there was no further flooding on a worldwide scale. The earth's topography remained virtually the same after that, and a large amount of water never again came upon the land.

As a result, the deluge in the days of Peleg became a significant milestone, as well as the prelude to more than four thousand years of additional world history that someday would culminate in the return of floodwaters to the north and the restoration of the earth to its former condition. At the end of this time period there were also to be many other concluding events, each one specifically detailed in scripture and all scheduled to occur in the latter days. A grand finale, as it were, was prearranged to take place at the end of the world.

An interesting note about these future occurrences is that two of them, traditionally regarded as mysterious and inexplicable, even legendary at times, turn out to be very closely associated with the division of the earth. At about the same time in the future, for example, when the waters of the great deep are driven back into the north countries, the famous conflict known as the Battle of Armageddon will take place in Palestine. Also descendants of the ten tribes of Israel, a group of people who have been lost for centuries in some remote and isolated place, will finally make their way back to modern civilization.

Certainly both of these events, occurring in close proximity to the end of the final deluge, are significant milestones in and of themselves and will be among the most remarkable in the earth's human history. Each will be part of a unique period of time, often referred to as the end of the world, which down through the ages has been the subject of frequent speculation and commentary, as well as religious prophecy!

A FINAL

Battle

In the book of Ezekiel in the Bible, there is a mysterious reference to Gog, the chief prince of Meshech and Tubal, who in the last days will lead a giant army out of the north country in a widespread attack on Palestine. At that time many other groups will join him, and together they will move across the land like a storm. The biblical record states that in those days it will be many nations of the world combined against the Jewish people who are living upon the mountains of Israel.

This will be the notorious Battle of Armageddon, occurring from the Plain of Esdraelon in the north all the way to the city of Jerusalem in the south. It is an event prophesied not only in the book of Ezekiel but in the books of Joel, Zechariah, and Revelation. It is also one of the least understood occurrences in the Bible, yet nevertheless one of the most important to take place in the latter days.

Very close in time to the final return of floodwaters in the north, this particular battle will be a part of the grand culmination of the earth's regular history. After all of the wars that have been fought down through the centuries, this will be the last one before the world finally comes to an end. Indeed, it is in this same time period that the Second Coming of Jesus Christ will occur and the earth will be renewed and restored to a paradisiacal glory!

In comparison with other wars, the Battle of Armageddon will in many ways be the worst conflict the world has ever seen. Although the weaponry and means of warfare might not always be highly sophisticated, the intensity of fighting will be unparalleled. In the words of the prophet Joel, "There hath not been ever the like, neither shall be any more after it, even to the years of many generations."[42]

At the time of this last great battle, the forces of Gog will come down from the north country out of the land called Magog, which traditionally is the same as ancient Scythia near the upper parts of the Black and Caspian Seas. In a modern world known for its high technology and scientific achievement, many of the invaders will appear as in days of old, "all of them riding upon horses, a great company, and a mighty army."[43]

This will not be just an ordinary invasion. The intent of the aggressor will be to conquer Israel and destroy it. The bitterness and hatred for the Jewish people, after building up in the Middle East for centuries, will suddenly break loose in a huge onslaught of mounted warriors. From many nations in different parts of the world, including Iran or ancient Persia, and Libya and Ethiopia, they will gather around Gog their leader, "all of them clothed with all sorts of armor, even a great company with bucklers and shields, all of them handling swords."[44] And in one gigantic thrust, the invading armies will cover the land like a cloud.

According to Joel's prophecy, it will be a time of great trouble, "a day of darkness and of gloominess, a day of clouds and of thick darkness. . . . A fire devoureth before them," the prophet says, "and behind them a flame burneth: the land is as the garden of Eden before them, and behind them a desolate wilderness; yea, and nothing shall escape them."[45]

But all of this will be to no avail, as far as Gog and his forces are concerned. Eventually, the Lord himself will intervene, and with a rain of hailstones, fire, and brimstone, he will bring the devastating invasion to an end. A countless number of men and animals will fall on that fateful day, and their dead bodies will cover the open fields.

Especially in Jerusalem in the south there will be a dramatic end to the battle. After being overrun by enemy forces, and at a time when everything appears to be lost, the Jewish people will be delivered in a spectacular and supernatural manner as the Lord Jesus Christ appears and stands upon the Mount of Olives across from the city.

At that moment, according to the book of Zechariah, the mount will cleave in two, one part shifting to the north and the other to the south, providing a miraculous pathway of escape. The captives will flee to the valley of the mountains, and much like the parting of the Red Sea when Moses led the Hebrews out of Egypt, a cataclysmic separation of land will now save a similar group, the embattled inhabitants of Jerusalem and the modern-day descendants of ancient Israel.

This one occurrence, apart from everything else, stands out above all others during the Battle of Armageddon. It is the surprising climax that will bring all fighting and aggression to an end. It is also the event, among many others, that will precede and announce the Second Coming of Jesus Christ and signal the beginning of the long-awaited Millennium!

But eventually, when all of this has happened and the fighting is completely over, still another event will occur that presents a grim and solemn epilogue. When everything has come to an end, and before the Jewish people begin clearing away the refuse and burying the dead, an unusual feast will take place in Palestine, one that is very graphically described in the Bible.

The Lord will invite every feathered fowl and every beast of the field to assemble themselves together upon the battleground for a great sacrifice that he has prepared for them. It will be an invitation to attend a banquet, as it were, and to eat at the royal table. In fact, this future event is referred to in scripture not only as the summons to a sacrifice but also as an invitation to attend the Lord's supper.

To all the fowls and beasts the Lord will say, "Come and gather yourselves together unto the supper of the great God."[46] "Assemble yourselves, and come; gather yourselves on every side to my sacrifice that I do sacrifice for you, even a great sacrifice upon the mountains of Israel, that ye may eat flesh and drink blood.

"Ye shall eat the flesh of the mighty, and drink the blood of the princes of the earth. . . . And ye shall eat fat till ye be full, and drink blood till ye be drunken, of my sacrifice which I have sacrificed for you. Thus ye shall be filled at my table with horses and chariots, with mighty men, and with all men of war, saith the Lord God."[47]

It is only after all of this has been accomplished that the people of Palestine will then start cleansing the land, clearing away the weapons and removing the dead. It will take seven months to bury Gog and his armies in a valley by the sea, and the weapons recovered from the battlegrounds will provide fuel to burn for seven years.

And finally, in addition to everything that has happened, the event pertaining to the time of Peleg is also scheduled to occur. Sometime in the vicinity of the Lord's Second Advent, floodwaters that divided the earth many hundreds of years ago will return to the north countries where they first appeared. At a designated signal and in response to a divine command, the seas and oceans will again greatly diminish, and land surfaces will revert to the way they were in the beginning.

In those days it will be the Lord himself who once more gives the final decrees. As recorded in scripture, he will stand upon the Mount of Olives and cause the mount to cleave apart, and also "upon the mighty ocean, even the great deep, and upon the islands of the sea," and his voice will be like thunder. He will speak to all nations and people and bring about vast changes in the earth's surface, transforming hills and valleys and causing mountains to crumble. And then once again during the general time period when all of this is taking place, the last deluge will finally come to a close, the final gathering of waters and the consummation of all floods!

"He shall command the great deep and it shall be driven back into the north countries, and the islands shall become one land. And the land of Jerusalem and the land of Zion shall be turned back into their own place, and the earth shall be like as it was in the days before it was divided."

Then will the end come, and also a new beginning. "And the Lord, even the Savior, shall stand in the midst of his people, and shall reign over all flesh."[48]

RETURN OF THE
Lost Tribes

At about the same time that the final floodwaters recede from the land, and some time preceding or following the Battle of Armageddon, another miraculous event will occur in the last days. The ten tribes of Israel, whose ancestors mysteriously disappeared many centuries ago and since then have remained hidden from the rest of society, will finally begin making their way from somewhere in the north country and heading southward toward an ancestral homeland.

Their first stop, as predicted in modern scripture, will be a place called Zion in the central part of the United States where they will meet with a group called the children of Ephraim. From there, according to another account, they will eventually continue their historic journey and arrive at a final destination in Palestine, at that time joining with others in fulfilling ancient prophecy and reclaiming the land of their first inheritance.

Certainly this will be a remarkable event, a modern exodus in which people once again respond to a divine command and make the long trek to a promised land. It will be the conclusion of almost three millennia of Israelite history that have long been characterized by mystery and uncertainty and today still remain a matter almost completely unknown. The true identity of the lost tribes, in fact, at least for most of their existence, has been a matter of secrecy and nondisclosure.

In retrospect, it was the ancestors of these people who once lived in the Kingdom of Israel, originating soon after the death of King Solomon and often referred to as the ten tribes. This kingdom, with a capital in the city of Samaria, was a counterpart to the Kingdom of Judah whose capital was in Jerusalem. Both groups were Israelites, the descendants of Abraham, Isaac, and Jacob.

But late in the eighth century BC, things suddenly changed as far as the Kingdom of Israel was concerned. The people were conquered by the Assyrians, and a large segment of the population was taken into captivity. At various sites in Media and upper Mesopotamia, the prisoners were resettled in new areas where they remained for more than a hundred years.

Then a certain number of them broke away and headed north, traveling extensively in an unknown land until they arrived at a distant location. There they vanished completely, never to be heard of again until some future time in the latter days.

Wherever these people are at present, they appear to have been existing for centuries as a separate and distinct group. An account in modern scripture, for example, tells of Jesus Christ visiting their civilization after his death and resurrection, at which time he referred to them as part of the "other sheep" he had spoken of while living in Palestine. And today, according to religious prophecies, they are still at some unknown location, awaiting the signal that will again take them out of some type of captivity, as it were, and start them moving toward a promised land.

Like the supernatural event at the Mount of Olives, the return of the ten tribes will also be a miraculous occurrence. What little is known about this mysterious group of people suggests extraordinary circumstances and phenomena. Indeed there is the suggestion in scripture that they will be coming from a remote and unusual place and that their reentry into modern-day society will be a dramatic one.

The implication, in fact, is that somewhere in the northern

part of the globe, sometimes referred to as the land of the north or the north country, is the same general area where the ten tribes allegedly disappeared and where their literal descendants someday will reappear. It is interesting also that these two events are in close proximity, within a reasonable number of miles, with two others in history, meaning the influx and recession of floods, and that the connection of all four events with the north counties is very possibly not just a coincidence but rather a strong implication that something of unusual importance has happened in the past and will again happen in the future.

At some undetermined time during the latter days, for example, most likely prior to the final gathering of waters, the tribes will emerge through a remarkable passageway much like the children of Israel when they passed through the Red Sea. Some kind of barrier composed of rock and ice will cleave apart before them, providing an escape from an unknown area to the outside world. And as in former times when Moses and Aaron went before the Hebrews, this latter-day group of Israelites will again be guided by the Lord and also led by prophets.

"And they who are in the north countries shall come in remembrance before the Lord; and their prophets shall hear his voice, and shall no longer stay themselves; and they shall smite the rocks, and the ice shall flow down at their presence. And an highway shall be cast up in the midst of the great deep."

"And they shall bring forth their rich treasures unto the children of Ephraim, my servants. And the boundaries of the everlasting hills shall tremble at their presence. And there shall they fall down and be crowned with glory, even in Zion, by the hands of the servants of the Lord, even the children of Ephraim."[49]

It was the tribe of Ephraim long ago that was one of the ten tribes conquered by the Assyrians. Because of the group's influence and leadership within the Kingdom of Israel, however, the name of the tribe was sometimes used exclusively in designating the entire kingdom. Following the conquest, for example, after thousands had been deported northward into the Assyrian Empire, the prophet Jeremiah mentioned this group collectively at one time by only one name: the "seed of Ephraim."

In speaking to the people of Judah in the south concerning a similar fate that would soon befall them, the prophet gave a solemn warning. "And I will cast you out of my sight," he said, quoting the Lord, "as I have cast out all your brethren, even the whole seed of Ephraim."[50]

These circumstances contribute significantly to the identity and importance of this particular tribe. The reasons for its unusual superiority are not entirely known, but the idea that it will play a strategic role in the return of the ten tribes is definitely implied.

At that time it will be Ephraim traveling from the north to meet people from the tribe of Ephraim in the south. In the city of Zion, also called the New Jerusalem, these two groups of an ancient birthright will once more join together in a historic reunion. The lineage that bound them together in the past will again reestablish them in the future as a great people and a dominant force in the coming Millennium.

It will be a period in history when the movement known as the gathering of Israel, so often mentioned in biblical and modern scripture, will rapidly start nearing the first stage of its conclusion. The house and family that began with Abraham, Isaac, and Jacob and that became famous when Moses led the Israelites out of Egypt, will be coming together from their long dispersion. And in a giant process of restoration, not only will the House of Israel eventually be reunited, but the earth itself will be changed and restored to the way it was in the beginning!

MODERN

Scripture

During a time of history when the regular affairs of the world start coming to a close, three events in particular stand out as important, all coinciding with the Second Advent of Jesus Christ. The Battle of Armageddon, the return of flood-waters to the north, and the reappearance of the lost tribes of Israel will all take place during the general time period when one part of the earth's existence is completed and another, known as the Millennium, begins.

This will be a time of great upheaval and transformation in which islands and continents again become one landmass. Massive earthquakes will occur, causing mountains to crumble and valleys to undergo transformation. All of this will be in direct fulfillment of ancient and modern prophecy.

Two prophecies especially are significant in connection with these events. They are found in a record of scripture called the Doctrine and Covenants and are valuable sources of information, providing insight into some very important questions, specifically those pertaining to the division of the earth.

Like other forms of scripture, this record is an accumulation of writings by a man who was regarded by his followers as a prophet. It was first published in 1835 and presently comprises 138 sections. Information concerning the earth's division, as well as that relating to the lost tribes, is found in section 133. Although quite brief, occupying only a small part of the entire account, the fifteen verses covering these two subjects are nevertheless among the most remarkable in both ancient and modern scripture. One who reads this material carefully, verses 20 through 34, might well conclude that something noticeably different is involved that is beyond the knowledge and capability of an ordinary man.

The Doctrine and Covenants, according to its title page, contains revelations given to a man named Joseph Smith who lived in the eastern and central parts of the United States during the first half of the nineteenth century. The original purpose of the book, as stated in the introduction, was to assist in establishing The Church of Jesus Christ of Latter-day Saints upon the earth and to direct its affairs as an institution. In addition, the record sets forth a detailed volume of religious principles and doctrine as well as various prophecies of things to come.

The two prophecies in the Doctrine and Covenants that are highly significant once again refer to the final deluge of floodwaters returning to its place of origin and also the ten tribes of Israel coming out of the north country. These particular scriptures, which are listed below, answer important historical questions and describe miraculous events that are yet to occur in the future, the central figure in all of them being the Lord Jesus Christ.

"For behold, he shall stand upon the mount of Olivet, and upon the mighty ocean, even the great deep, and upon the islands of the sea, and upon the land of Zion. And he shall utter his voice out of Zion, and he shall speak from Jerusalem, and his voice shall be heard among all people; And it shall be a voice as the voice of many waters, and as the voice of a great thunder, which shall break down the mountains, and the valleys shall not be found.

"He shall command the great deep, and it shall be driven back into the north countries, and the islands shall become one land; And the land of Jerusalem and the land of Zion shall be turned back into their own place, and the earth shall be like as it was in the days before it was divided.

"And the Lord, even the Savior, shall stand in the midst of his people, and shall reign over all flesh.

"And they who are in the north countries shall come in remembrance before the Lord; and their prophets shall hear his voice, and shall no longer stay themselves; and they shall smite the rocks, and the ice shall flow down at their presence. And an highway shall be cast up in the midst of the great deep.

"Their enemies shall become a prey unto them, And in the barren deserts there shall come forth pools of living water; and the parched ground shall no longer be a thirsty land. And they shall bring forth their rich treasures unto the children of Ephraim, my servants. And the boundaries of the everlasting hills shall tremble at their presence.

"And there shall they fall down and be crowned with glory, even in Zion, by the hands of the servants of the Lord, even the children of Ephraim. And they shall be filled with songs of everlasting joy. Behold, this is the blessing of the everlasting God upon the tribes of Israel, and the richer blessing upon the head of Ephraim and his fellows."[51]

Certainly it would be difficult to think of many occurrences having greater significance and impact than these! The recession of large amounts of water and the return of the ten tribes, much like the Battle of Armageddon, are almost beyond comprehension when compared with normal everyday events. Again it is a reminder that the concluding scenes of world history will unquestionably be highly miraculous and extraordinary.

"Let the waters under the heaven be gathered together unto one place, and let the dry land appear!" This was the divine command on the morning of Creation, and comparable words are implied at the end of the great Flood during the time of Noah. And likewise, a similar edict will be given when the waters that divided the earth in the days of Peleg are again driven back into the north countries.

During the same general time period, very likely before the Second Coming of Jesus Christ, the descendants of the ten tribes of Israel will come out of a northern area, released after many centuries from a long seclusion. In very few places is there a description more graphic and remarkable than that which depicts the return of these ten lost tribes.

All of this once again is found in the book that has come to be known as the Doctrine and Covenants. Only in this one record is there an account of these latter-day events. If it were not for this particular book of scripture containing the revelations of Joseph Smith, the important details pertaining to these occurrences would probably still be unknown.

But the book does exist, and according to the testimony of many people, it comes from a divine source and is regarded as scripture. For more than a hundred and fifty years it has been published in a variety of languages and distributed throughout the world. Although its authenticity so far has been recognized by relatively few, its contents make it clear that the revelations involved are for the benefit of all people.

Moreover, because the material in section 133 especially has provided such important insight into difficult problems and questions, it gives additional credibility to other things that Joseph Smith did and taught. The boldness of the text and the tenor of its content both suggest that something beyond ordinary experience is present and that the man who said he obtained new knowledge through divine revelation was in reality telling the truth. There is much more to the Doctrine and Covenants, in other words, than just an important religious document.

And when the day comes that all of this is finally confirmed, if things actually turn out as described, then will everyone know, as Isaiah and Ezekiel said of old, that "a marvelous work and a wonder" has been revealed to the people and that indeed "a prophet hath been among them!"[52]

AN EXTRAORDINARY

Revelation

In addition to the 133rd section of the Doctrine and Covenants, which describes the end of a deluge and the return of the ten lost tribes of Israel, another part of the book is equally important, particularly as it pertains to the controversial subject of chronology. The area designated as the 77th section, for example, gives an extraordinary religious prophecy, including the general time period of the Second Coming of Jesus Christ, and tells for the first time how various events in the future fit chronologically into the stream of world history.

The scripture is highly significant because it comes at a time when biblical scholars are far from any kind of consensus as to when certain events and phenomena took place during the time of the Old Testament, particularly those occurring prior to the first millennium before Christ. There is also the question of how many years were in specific time periods, such as the life spans of the ancient prophets and patriarchs. Moreover, a continuing problem is synchronizing things that happened in the Bible with corresponding secular accounts, at the same time attempting to reconcile a variety of differences in regard to chronology.

In view of this, the 77th section of the Doctrine and Covenants becomes the primary reason for using the King James

Version of the Bible, rather than any other version, in discussing the man named Peleg and the division of the earth, one of the reasons being that the two records are compatible chronologically. The information that the section contains is briefly stated and is the result of a revelation that Joseph Smith reportedly received in regard to certain questions pertaining to the book of Revelation in the New Testament. Of particular importance is a statement declaring that the earth's human history up to the present time consists of six, one-thousand year periods, establishing the time of Adam and Eve in the Garden of Eden at about 4,000 years before Christ, a date similar to that in the King James chronology.

In a present time of continuing controversy concerning the beginning of human life upon the earth and the extent of associated world history, the alleged revelation is significant. It defines a starting point and frame of reference pertaining to the human experience, a point that had been introduced almost two hundred years previously but until the time of Joseph Smith was never confirmed.

During the years 1650 to 1654, an archbishop named James Ussher, who was an Anglican prelate of Ireland, published computations which he had made on the chronology of the Old Testament, using the Hebrew text of the Bible as the basis for his research. Among his conclusions at the time was the declaration that the creation of the earth took place in 4004 BC, approximately 4,000 years before the birth of Jesus Christ.

The Ussher chronology appeared to be logical and systematic, dividing human history into several meaningful periods. The first two thousand years covered the time from Adam to Abraham, followed by another two thousand years up to the time of Christ. Two thousand more years then led up to the end of the sixth millennium. It was a system often accepted by scholars and public alike for more than two centuries and was listed in the King James Bible as marginal dates and footnotes.

But during the nineteenth century, the computations created by Ussher began to lose credibility for one reason or another, and today his chronology generally is not used. Dates often do not synchronize with events in secular history nor fit into the broad scheme of things chronologically. It is ironic, therefore, after all of this time, that a certain scripture should suddenly appear in the time of Joseph Smith that was compatible with an Ussher-type chronology, especially in view of the fact that the religious and scientific communities still do not favor it.

The scripture refers to an unusual book in the fifth chapter of the book of Revelation that was sealed on the back with seven seals. Concerning the contents of this book, the 77th section gives the following information. "We are to understand," the scripture says, "that it contains the revealed will, mysteries, and works of God; the hidden things of his economy concerning this earth during the seven thousand years of its continuance, or its temporal existence."[53]

In very few words, the information contained in this scripture divulges the extent of the world's entire human history from the very beginning in the Garden of Eden to the end of the biblical Millennium. In a remarkable statement, it also confirms how many years have been involved so far in the earth's "continuance, or its temporal existence," referring to the first six thousand years. And regardless of what public reaction might be to this kind of information, in view of its abruptness and unusual conciseness and brevity, as well as its bold assertion concerning chronology, it stands as a revolutionary and unqualified statement, the authority of which is the revelation attributed to Joseph Smith as recorded in the Doctrine and Covenants.

This one statement, in fact, if accepted as truth, revolutionizes the thinking within current dating systems pertaining to the Old Testament and again gives credibility to the computations of James Ussher who lived in Ireland 400 years ago. At the same time, it implies that certain changes and adjustments in both secular and biblical records will eventually be made, reconciling various differences in regard to chronology. This could result in adjusting secular history to fit prophecy at times, rather than vice versa as has sometimes been the case.

In addition, an important statement is made in the 77th section regarding the opening of the seven seals mentioned in chapters six and eight of the book of Revelation. In connection with such seals and their relationship to chronology, the scripture records the following. "We are to understand that the first seal contains the things of the first thousand years," referring again to the earth and the seven thousand years of its continuance, "and the second also of the second thousand years, and so on until the seventh."[54]

Only meager information is given in the book of Revelation as to what happened when most of the seals were opened, but it does refer to the duration of human life upon the earth, which once again is seven thousand years. In other words, the Bible itself gives significant confirmation concerning how long the earth has been the scene of human habitation.

The 77th section of the Doctrine and Covenants is also an extremely important revelation on what will take place in the beginning of the seventh millennium, a period where the term "in the beginning" might refer to a very considerable length of time, even to the extent of a large part of a century. This is a period that will occur just prior to the commencement of that part of history which will be known as the biblical Millennium.

Of particular significance is the mystical reference to the sounding of trumpets by the seven angels as recorded in the eighth chapter of the book of Revelation. In connection with this event, the modern scripture in the Doctrine and Covenants correlates the seventh day of the earth's creation with the seventh thousand years of its temporal existence and tells specifically what will happen at the very beginning of that final period. Again it is an extraordinary revelation.

"We are to understand that as God made the world in six days," says the scripture, "and on the seventh day he finished his work, and sanctified it, and also formed man out of the dust of the earth, even so, in the beginning of the seventh thousand years will the Lord God sanctify the earth and complete the salvation of man, and judge all things, and shall redeem all things, except that which he hath not put into his power, when he shall have sealed all things, unto the end of all things; and the sounding of the trumpets of the seven angels [is] the preparing and finishing of his work, in the beginning of the seventh thousand years—the preparing of the way before the time of his coming."[55]

In the commencement of the seventh millennium, therefore, whatever length of time this comes to mean, events of tremendous importance will occur, including the sanctification of the earth and the processes of final judgment and redemption. All things relating to the previous six thousand years will be brought to a close. But the remarkable revelation given in the 77th section mentions one thing further: the announcement of the Second Coming of Jesus Christ and the outstanding occurrences immediately preceding his return. The sounding of the trumpets of the seven angels, in other words, mentioned in the book of Revelation, dramatically describes the final events and preparations that will occur during the beginning of the seventh millennium, after which the Second Coming and the biblical Millennium will then take place.

All of this could result in a variety of time schedules, of course, and the only thing definite is that the "preparing and finishing" of the Lord's work "before the time of his coming" will happen sometime in the beginning of the seventh thousand years. This means that a year such as 2005 could very easily evolve into 2015 or 2035 before the Second Coming, or even a period of time well beyond that. Nothing is more definite than what is given in the present revelation and scripture. It is also a reminder of words spoken by Jesus himself at one

time during his earthly ministry, words spoken to his disciples which today still come ringing down from the past. "But
of that day and hour knoweth no man," he said, "no, not the
angels of heaven, but my Father only."[56]

Epilogue

In conclusion, it is a matter of great importance, according to the many signs that have been given, that the world has now reached an advanced stage of progression and entered what has often been called the latter days. In an era sometimes known as the Dispensation of the Fulness of Times, events are currently taking place that will conclude the first part of the earth's recorded history and finally usher in the Millennium, all of which has been foretold by ancient and modern prophets and recorded in scripture.

Among the many prophecies, of course, is the one pertaining to the division of the earth that states that a giant flood dating back to the Tower of Babel is soon to be consummated and that floodwaters will return to their original source. The deluge that occurred during the time of Peleg will recede by way of the north countries, after which a former landmass will be restored. Then in preparation for what is to follow, the earth will be renewed and returned to its previous status and glory.

In connection with this particular prophecy, along with its many implications, a subject that keeps coming back again and again is Peleg, the man referred to in the Bible at the time the earth was divided. Among all those that might be mentioned, he is the one person associated with this momentous event that has received such a small amount of attention in history.

It is his name in the books of Genesis and 1 Chronicles that signifies a watercourse or a type of division and hints strongly that it had something to do with a large deluge of water. Regardless of who he was as an individual, the name he went by obviously designated an event of great significance and importance. As a consequence, he occupies a unique position in ancient scripture.

Yet at the same time, his story also contains a definite irony and contradiction. Against the vast background of history, for example, and the predictions and prophecies of things to come, any serious consideration of the man named Peleg appears relatively minor and unimportant. Only for his name is he recognized, in other words, and not for anything notable that he did. As a figure in biblical history, he is virtually unknown.

And in reality such a thing is not surprising. Maybe that is the way things actually were during his lifetime because Peleg himself apparently had no higher status than anyone else in the patriarchal line, much less, in fact, than people such as Adam, Enoch, and Noah. His own personal significance might have been nothing more than common or ordinary, other than being associated by name with the division of the earth mentioned in the Bible.

Modern prophecy makes a brief reference to the division but says almost nothing about Peleg. The conclusion, therefore, based on what is recorded in scripture, is that only the occurrence was important and not so much the man.

But Peleg will still remain a person of mystery and fascination because of his association with such a famous event. In the brief genealogical accounts that contain his name, there is only a hint of importance, yet it is enough to set him apart from all of the individuals surrounding him.

Of course, the main thing is that something significant occurred during his lifetime that affected the lives of all mankind. A radical change in geography took place that influenced the affairs of every nation, kindred, tongue, and people. But in the process, Peleg still gained his unexpected recognition, and even though he was an innocent bystander when the event took place, he nevertheless became its famous contemporary and namesake.

Yet ironically it is also the event itself that has remained so much in obscurity down through the centuries. Despite the fact that something immensely important occurred in those days, the world is still very unaware and complacent about anything having to do with a so-called division of the earth. The documentation for this outstanding occurrence is so limited that it normally attracts only brief attention. It stands almost undetected within a large context of unrelated material. But still it is there, hidden away and appearing very unexpectedly in the genealogies and historical narratives of biblical scripture!

Although it is interrelated with some of the most important events in the Bible, it is mentioned in only two isolated places and in most ways continues to be a mystery. Again it is as though a tremendous thought had been inserted between two relatively unimportant ideas for an unknown purpose, a thought unintended to be fully divulged and understood until the latter days. Not until the end of the world, in fact, at a time spoken of by the ancient prophets, might the complete story ever be known.

And on that occasion, when the grand denouement of human affairs finally takes place, when the surface of the earth is transformed and a new world prepares to enter the Millennium, the name of Peleg once again could very well be in the forefront, signifying the man whose birth coincided with a very crucial event in history and whose life and true identity are still very much in question!

References
AND Comments

Note: The King James Version of the Bible, the Book of Mormon, the Doctrine and Covenants, and the Pearl of Great Price are standard works of The Church of Jesus Christ of Latter-day Saints.

1. Genesis 5:24.
2. Josha 10:13.
3. Genesis 10:25. See also I Chronicles 1:19.
4. Genesis 10:30.
5. Ibid., 11:4.
6. Genesis 10:9.
7. Flavius Josephus, *The Complete Works of Josephus*, Book 1. Translated by William Whiston. (Grand Rapids, Michigan: Kregel Publications, 1981), 30.
8 .Ibid., 30.
9. 1 Chronicles 1:19.
10. Genesis 10:5.
11. Ibid., 10:32.
12. Doctrine and Covenants 133:23-24.
13. Genesis 1:2, 9-10.
14. Ibid., 7:11, 24.
15. Another explanation of what might have occurred is the rising terrain theory. If the ocean floor were raised up, for example, it would displace a large amount of water onto land surfaces. Conversely, sinking terrain would cause the water to drain off again.
16. Doctrine and Covenants 133:23.

17. Ibid., 133:38-39. See also Revelation 14:7.

18. Ibid., 133:23-24.

19. Robert Davidson, *The Cambridge Bible Commentary*, Genesis 1–11 (London: Cambridge University Press, 1973), 20.

The idea of large volumes of water existing beneath the earth's surface is also suggested in Psalm 136:6. The text of this verse appears as follows in The New English Bible and the King James Version, respectively: (1) "He laid the earth upon the waters." (2) "To him that stretched the earth above the waters." Exodus 20:4 possibly contains a related scripture.

20. One way of visualizing a huge amount of subterranean water is to compare it with water already existing on the earth's surface. The oceans at present are said to cover nearly three-fourths of the globe with an average depth of about two miles, yet despite their tremendous size and dominating ratio in respect to land, they are still relatively just a small film, the same of which might be said of subterranean water.

"If a sphere three feet in diameter representing the earth were dipped in water and withdrawn," to cite an analogy, "the wet film adhering to its surface would correctly depict the oceanic depth" (Richard Webster, ed. *The Volume Library* [New York: Educator's Association, Inc., 1946], 1110). In addition, such an analogy suggests that vast expanses of subterranean water, at whatever locations they might exist, also in reality are only a small film or smear, as it were, in regard to their overall extent and volume.

21. In connection with the subterranean theory, there are at least three others that might explain the origin of floods: (1) upheavals beneath the sea that push up the ocean floor and displace water onto the land, (2) sinking terrain on land surfaces that allows a large influx of water from seas and oceans, and (3) divine intervention in which water is supernaturally multiplied.

22. Henry Hampton Halley, *Halley's Bible Handbook* (Grand Rapids, Michigan: Zondervan Publishing House, 1965), 76-77. Note: There are many different translations of the Gilgamesh Epic in which this particular reference is found, but the one mentioned by Halley is especially descriptive. However, he does not quote his source. Other translations include those by John Gardner and John Maier, Alexander Heidel, and Maureen Gallery Kovacs.

23. Doctrine and Covenants 133:26.

24. Ibid., 133:20-26.

25. Genesis 10:25.

26. Ibid., 11:1-2.

27. This kind of situation is also alluded to in a verse from modern scripture. The Book of Mormon, for example, referring to Lucifer or the devil, states that it was he "who put it into the hearts of the people to build a tower sufficiently high that they might get to heaven." (See Helaman 6:28.)

28. Genesis 9:11, 13.

29. David M. Rohl, *Pharaohs and Kings, A Biblical Quest* (New York: Crown Publishers, Inc., 1995), 8, 9, 11, 60, 80, 107, 138-39, and 143.

Note: Another example of reduced dynastic time periods can be seen in the diminishing figures by which scholars over the years have dated the unification of upper and lower Egypt under Menes, regarded as the first bona fide Egyptian pharaoh. L. "Champollion, 5867 BC; Lesueur, 5770; Bokh, 5702; Unger, 5613; Mariette, 5004; Brugsch, 4455; Lauth, 4157; Chabas, 4000; Lepsius, 3892; Bunsen, 3623; Eduard Meyer, 3180; Wilkinson, 2320; Palmer, 2224. Breasted dates Menes at 3400, George Steindorff at 3200, and the newest research at 2900." C.W. Ceram, *Gods, Graves, and Scholars* (New York: Alfred A. Knopf, 1953), 122-123.

Note: The idea of a theoretical decrease of the antediluvian period and a similar increase of the postdiluvian can be seen in certain population figures from the Old Testament. The ten antediluvian patriarchs, for example, as they are listed according to generations in the King James Version of the Bible, are shown below. (See Genesis 5:1-32; 11:10-26.) The format is that Adam lived 130 years and begat Seth, Seth lived 105 years and begat Enos, and so forth. (The numbers in parentheses indicate total lifetimes.)

Adam 130 (930)

Seth 105 (912)

Enos 90 (905)

Cainan 70 (910)

Mahalaleel 65 (895)

Jared 162 (962)

Enoch 65 (430)

Methuselah 187 (969)

Lamech 182 (777)

Noah 502 (950)

By subtracting 800 years, in one way or another, from the lengthy lifetimes of the first ten patriarchs and then adding those years proportionately to the eight patriarchs following Shem, a traditional Flood date of about 2350 BC might be revised to read 3150 BC, which hypothetically and historically would place the date very close to the beginning of the Egyptian dynasties.

Shem 100 (610)

Arphaxad 35 (438)

Salah 30 (433)

Eber 34 (464)

Peleg 30 (239)

Reu 32 (239)

Serug 30 (230)

Nehor 29 (148)

Terah 70 (205)

Abraham

30. It is important to remember that the Tower of Babel was not finished prior to the confusion of tongues and the dispersion of people.

31. Genesis 1:9.

32. Ibid., 7:4 and 8:1.

33. Luke 8:25.

34. Proverbs 8:29.

35. Doctrine and Covenants 133:23-24.

36. Acts 3:20-21.

37. Isaiah 40:4.

38. Doctrine and Covenants 133:24.

Note: The turning back of the land of Jerusalem and the land of Zion into their own place apparently refers to the time just prior to the Millennium when the earth will be restored geologically and geographically to the way it was in the beginning. The recession of the deluge that had occurred during the days of Peleg would account for many changes in geography, but for the geology of the earth to return to the way it was before it was divided, involving all kinds of alterations and transformations, a tremendous cataclysm of some kind would need to occur, one without parallel or precedent.

Such an event, or one very much like it, could very well be the massive earthquake scheduled to take place in the future in connection with the Battle of Armageddon. At that time there will be "a great earthquake," according to the book of Revelation, "such as was not since men were upon the earth, so mighty an earthquake and so great" (Revelation 16:18).

This particular event, and undoubtedly many others that are similar, could produce the rocking of the earth that will move everything back into an original place and location, including the land of Jerusalem and the land of Zion. Much will likely occur geographically and hydraulically during this time period as well in order to restore the earth to the way it was before it was divided in the days of Peleg.

39. Genesis 10:32.

40. Ibid., 11:8-9.

41. 2 Nephi 10:21. See The Book of Mormon.

42. Joel 2:2.

43. Ezekiel 38:15.

44. Ibid., 38:4-5.

45. Joel 2:2-3.

46. Revelation 19:17.

47. Ezekiel 39:20.

48. Doctrine and Covenants 133:23-25.

49. Ibid., 133:26-27, 30-32.

50. Jeremiah 7:15.

51. Doctrine and Covenants 133:20-34.

52. Isaiah 29:14 and Ezekiel 33:33.

53. Doctrine and Covenants 77:6.

54. Doctrine and Covenants 77:7.

55. Doctrine and Covenants 77:12.

56. Matthew 24:36.

ABOUT THE *Author*

Clay McConkie is a native of Utah. He is a teacher by occupation, having taught in the Salt Lake City schools for thirty years. He received a BA from Brigham Young University and an MS and PhD from the University of Utah. He and his wife reside in Provo, Utah, and are the parents of four children.

He is also the author of *One Flesh, The Gathering of the Waters, The Ten Lost Tribes, In Ephraim's Footsteps, 600 BC,* and *In His Father's Image,* and *The Final Countdown.*

PORTRAIT DRAWINGS

John McConkie is an architect residing in Salt Lake City. He received a BS and an MS from the University of Utah. He and his wife are the parents of five children.